MW01243405

HITTIN' THE TRA

Day Hiking Trails of
Bayfield County

By Rob Bignell

Atiswinic Press · Ojai, Calif.

DAY HIKING TRAILS OF BAYFIELD COUNTY

A GUIDEBOOK IN THE
HITTIN' THE TRAIL: WISCONSIN SERIES

Copyright Rob Bignell, 2014

Atiswinic Press
Ojai, Calif. 93023
hikeswithtykes.com/hittinthetrail_home.html

ISBN 978-0-9896723-9-9

Cover design by Rob Bignell
Cover photo of Houghton Point near Washburn

Manufactured in the United States of America
First printing November 2014

DEDICATION

For Kieran

"When life becomes too fast, I find relief at last/
Out in the country."
– Three Dog Night, "Out in the Country"

Table of Contents

Introduction

I magine a place where you can hike sandy beaches and enjoy fantastic vistas of the world's largest freshwater lake, a place of towering pines that bald eagles fly over and black bears scamper under, a place where you can explore sea caves or hike across billion-year-old red rock. The place is real – it's called Bayfield County, Wisconsin.

If Wisconsin were a mitten, Bayfield County would be the peak of the four fingers. With much of it a peninsula, it boasts more shoreline on Lake Superior than any other Wisconsin county.

Because of this and other natural wonders, it's also a popular tourism destination, attracting skiers, boaters, campers and sightseers. It also offers dozens of miles of trails for those who love hiking.

Communities

Consisting mainly of forestland and lakeshore, each Bayfield County village feels like a quaint throwback to years past. Only one of them boasts a population close to 3000 people.

Ten villages can be found here, with the majority of them hugging the lakeshore or a county line.

Starting with the top destination and heading clockwise around the county, those communities include Bayfield, Washburn, a smidgen of Ashland, Drummond, Cable, Iron River, Port Wing, Herbster, Cornucopia, and Red Cliff.

Bayfield

Though a small village of little more than 500 people, you wouldn't know that when visiting in summer and early autumn. During weekend festivals, 40,000 people can descend upon Bayfield.

The village is named for Henry Bayfield, a British Royal Topographic Engineer, who explored this region in 1822-23. Today, the Bayfield Maritime Museum and Bayfield Heritage Museum pay homage to him and the region's colorful history. The annual Apple Fest, held the first weekend in October, and the Race Week Regatta, held in early July, attract tourists from multiple states. On other weekends, the fine weather, port to the Apostle Islands, and several art galleries achieves the same.

Madeline Island-La Pointe-Apostle Islands

Though technically not in Bayfield County, the main way most people access Madeline Island, its village of La Pointe, and the rest of the Apostle Islands, is through Bayfield on a 20-minute ferry ride – or during winter by driving on an ice road over frozen Lake Superior.

Tiny La Pointe in turn serves as the main launch

point to reach the other 21 Apostle Islands that lay north of Bayfield County in Lake Superior. Madeline Island, however, is not part of the Apostle Island National Lakeshore, and it's the only Apostle Island with private residences. The island and its Big Bay State Park are popular enough that many visitors never leave it for the national lakeshore.

Washburn

The county seat, Washburn also is the county's largest town at more than 2100 people. Sitting on the lakeshore, it was named after the former state governor who founded the town. Though known for tourism today, at one time is was home to a DuPont explosives plant.

Ashland

While most of this city of 8,600-plus sits in Ashland County, a bit of it crosses into Bayfield County. The town curves about Chequamegon Bay and was once a major port from which ore was shipped. A major draw today to the town today is the Northern Great Lakes Visitor Center, which is in Bayfield County.

Drummond

In the southcentral part of county is this town of little more than 500 people. Entirely surrounded by the Chequamegon National Forest, it's a natural center for outdoors activities.

Cable

In southern Bayfield County sits this village of some 800-plus, which the American Hiking Society named a charter "Trail Town USA" and for good reason: To Cable's north and east is the Chequamegon National Forest while to the south and east is the St. Croix National Scenic Riverway along the Namekagon River tributary, making the community a major gateway to outdoors activities in Bayfield County.

Among the village's annual events is the American Birkebeiner cross-country skiing race, which starts here and ends in nearby Hayward. Cable also is the finish line for the annual Chequamegon Fat Tire Festival mountain bike race.

Iron River

Moving up the west side of the county, in the southern corner is tucked Iron River, Bayfield County's second largest city with more than a thousand residents. Its main attractions are the Brule River State Forest in neighboring Douglas County and the Chequamegon National Forest to the east. The annual Blueberry Festival and Bayfield County Fair are held here each summer.

Port Wing-Herbster

North of Iron River on the Bayfield Peninsula along the Lake Superior shoreline is Port Wing and to the northeast Herbster. Both villages are unincorporated. Each relies on tourism and to a lesser extent fishing, lumbering and agriculture as their mainstays (Note: In this volume, hiking trails for both villages appear in the Iron River listings).

Cornucopia

Heading northeast up the peninsula's western shoreline is the unincorporated community of Cornucopia. It is near a mainland portion of the Apostle Islands National Lakeshore, which features the Mawikwe Bay Sea Caves.

Red Cliff

Circling around the top of the Bayfield Peninsula is the mainland portion of the national lakeshore. On the western shore is the village of Red Cliff, which serves as the Red Cliff Band of Lake Superior Chippewa's administrative center. Fewer than a thousand people live on the Red Cliff reservation.

The trails in this book are listed by the community that they cluster around. Those communities, in turn, are listed clockwise starting with Bayfield, in the order described above.

Attractions

Visitors to Bayfield County can enjoy a number of major recreational areas. The Chequamegon National Forest's western reach stretches across the county's southern and center section. A small portion of the Apostle Island National Lakeshore sits on the Bayield Peninsula with access to the rest of the National Park Service unit's scenic and often unspoiled islands primarily from Bayfield and La Pointe. Big Bay State Park – in Ashland County on Madeline Island – offers an intimate encounter with Lake Superior; most visiting the state park do so by first passing through Bayfield. Brule River State Forest, also just across the county line, lets visitors explore a waterway that at one time flowed out of Lake Superior rather than into it.

Two major trails cut through the county. The North Country National Scenic Trail, which rambles 4600 miles across seven states from New York to North Dakota, runs in Bayfield County between the southeast corner in the Chequamegon National Forest and south of Iron River on its way through the Brule River State Forest. The Tri-County Corridor Trail heads between Ashland and Superior in neighboring Douglas County, paralleling U.S. Hwy. 2 in Bayfield County.

How to Get There

From western Wisconsin and southern Minnesota, U.S. Hwy. 63 offers the best access to Bayfield County. The highway runs from Interstate 94 north, entering the county near Cable on its way to that village and Drummond before terminating west of Ashland.

From northern Minnesota, U.S. Hwy. 2 enters Wisconsin in Superior then enters Bayfield County at Iron River. Wis. Hwy. 13 also runs from south of Superior to and then along the Bayfield Peninsula shoreline.

From northeastern Wisconsin and Michigan's Upper Peninsula, U.S. Hwy 2 runs through Ashland and east-west across Bayfield County to Iron River.

Southeastern Wisconsin and Illinois residents can reach Bayfield County via Hwy. 13, which heads north from U.S. Hwy. 10 in Marshfield through Park Falls into Ashland. In Bayfield County, Hwy. 13 loops off Hwy. 2 and around the Bayfield Peninsula through Washburn, Bayfield, Red Cliff, Cornucopia, Herbster and Port Wing before swinging into Douglas County and ending just south of Superior.

When to Visit

Outdoors activities abound year around in Bayfield County. The best months to day hike Bayfield County, though, are May through September. Depending on the year, April and October also can be pleasant.

As with the rest of Wisconsin, summers are humid, especially July and August, though this typically is only the case for Bayfield County's inland areas. Rain also can occur during the afternoon even when the morning is sunny, so always check the weather forecast before heading out.

November through March usually is too cold for day hiking. Once snow falls, trails usually are used for cross-country skiing, snowmobiling or snow-shoeing. Early spring often means muddy trails thanks to snowmelt and rainfall.

Maps

Maps showing hiking trails, campgrounds, parking lots and other facilities are available online at: *http://hikeswithtykes.com/headintothecabin_trailma ps.html.*

Featured Trails

B ayfield County offers a diverse array of ecosystems and experiences for hikers to enjoy and discover. In this section, trails are listed by the county's major villages or attractions, going clockwise beginning with Bayfield. Following it is Madeline Island, Apostle Islands National Lakeshore, Washburn, Ashland, Drummond, Cable, Iron River (including Port Wing and Herbster) and the Cornucopia-Red Cliff region.

Bayfield

When most people visit Bayfield County, this picturesque village is their destination. Given the number of attractions surrounding Bayfield, that shouldn't come as a surprise. Located on scenic Lake Superior, it's the main port for reaching Madeline Island and the Apostle Islands National Lakeshore.

The Chequamegon National Forest, Bayfield County Forest, and Nourse Sugarbush State Natural Area all are only a few miles away. Because of this, more than a dozen day hiking trails can be found in or near the village.

Brownstone Trail

Day hikers can enjoy the Lake Superior shoreline along the Brownstone Trail in Bayfield.

The partially urban hike makes for a scenic 5.2-miles round trip walk and offers the popular tourist village significant public access to the lakeshore.

Park in historic downtown Bayfield or in the lot next to trailhead, which is on South Third Street south of Manypenny Avenue. From the lot, the trail angles southwest.

An abandoned Chicago and North Western Railway bed converted into a hiking trail, the line used to run from north of Bayfield to Washburn. Thanks to its train days, its surface is dirt and gravel and fairly even.

The trail first passes a marina. In addition to sailboats, sometime during the hike you're likely see the ferry leaving Bayfield or coming in from LaPointe en route between mainland and Madeline Island.

If short on time or energy, you can turn around at Lakeshore Drive (which later becomes Chequamegon Road) for a 1.5-mile round trip.

But the most scenic part of the hike is ahead as the trail continues onward curving between the water and Lakeshore Drive. You'll soon encounter the brownstone cliffs of the Lake Superior shoreline.

The sandstones settled there about a billion years ago when northeastward-flowing braided streams deposited sediment. In some sections of the Bayfield Peninsula, the typically red sandstone is up 4300 feet thick. It's entirely devoid of fossils.

In 1869, companies quarried the Bayfield area and some of the surrounding Apostle Islands for the brownstone. From there it was shipped to several Midwestern cities, including Chicago, Detroit, Milwaukee, Cincinnati and Kansas City for building construction. You also can see it locally; Washburn's Main Street museum, which at one time was a bank, and Ashland's Wheeler Hall at Northland College both use brownstone quarried in the region.

Thanks to the cliffs, the trail becomes quieter. This section of the hike also offers great views of sailboats on the lake and of Madeline Island in the distance.

The trail ends at Pikes Bay Marina and Port Superior. Beautiful sailing yachts often can be spotted nearby on Salmo Bay. After reaching the marina, retrace your steps back to downtown Bayfield.

The trail is popular with bicyclists, so step aside when two-wheelers pass. Also, stay on the trail except in designated areas, as it crosses privately-owned property.

Jerry Jolly Hiking Trail segment
Bayfield County Forest

Day hikers can explore Wisconsin's northern-most ecosystem on a segment of the Jerry Jolly Hiking Trail near Bayfield.

The Jerry Jolly is part of the Pike's Creek and Mt. Ashwabay Trail Network, a set of ski trails winding through a thousand acres of Bayfield County Forest and the Nourse Sugarbush Natural Area. The segment described here runs 1.1-miles round trip.

To reach the trailhead, take Wis. Hwy. 13 south from Bayfield, turning right/west onto County Road

J. In short order, the county highway becomes Star Route Road. After passing the Old Corny Road intersection, look for signs pointing out the parking lot for the Jerry Jolly trails on the right/south.

From the lot, head south on the stem trail for 0.31 miles. Along the way, the trail crosses a tributary to Pike's Creek.

The trails sit in the Superior Coastal Plain ecosystem, which includes the northern portions of Bayfield, Douglas, Ashland and Iron counties as well as the Apostle Islands. While much of the Bayfield Peninsula consists of pine barrens – areas of sandy soil that support mainly pine and scrub oak – Lake Superior greatly influences the coastal plain's climate. Winters are warmer, summers are cooler, and more rain and snow falls here than inland.

Because of that, a good mix of aspen birch and other hardwoods reside alongside pines and fir-spruce more common to the boreal forests farther north.

Another factor influencing the Pike's Creek climate is the Bayfield Peninsula's hilliness, which contrasts with the flatness of the pine barrens to the southwest. Evidence of the hilly terrain comes on the Jerry Jolly Trial just after the third trail junction, when the stem gains elevation for about 0.12 miles. At the fifth junction, take the trail heading left/ northeast, and for the next 0.06 miles the trail descends the hill.

Before pioneers settled this region, the Superior

Coastal Plain largely supported a boreal forest. Marten, fisher, beaver, caribou and gray wolf all thrived there. Once the old growth trees were cut, however, aspen-birch took over, and so the wild-life also changed. Today, white-tailed deer and smaller mammals, such as squirrel, chipmunks, rabbits and voles dominate the wooded landscape.

At the next junction, the trail reaches Jerry's Meadow Loop. Go right/east as wrapping around a small meadow for 0.25 miles.

Meadows such as this are extremely rare in the coastal plain. Often these grassy areas are aband-oned farmland pastures and fields.

At the next junction, the trail leaves the meadow for the stem you came in on. Go right/north on the stem for 0.25 miles.

Despite the large-scale disappearance of the coastal plain's boreal forest, birds from those Canadian woodlands migrate here some winters when food is not as plentiful in their northern homes. Skiers on the trail will hear or see owls that wouldn't be spotted during summer.

Upon reaching the next trail junction, for a little variety go right/northeast onto a small 0.12-mile loop. The loop returns to the stem trail farther ahead; at that junction, continue right/north back to the parking lot.

The trail is named for Jerry J. Jolly, a long-time Bayfield area outdoorsman. In 2007, the Jerry Jolly Hiking Trail was dedicated in his honor. Because of his middle initial, sometimes maps and brochures refer to the trail as the "Jerry Jay Jolly Trail."

One last note: By midsummer, parts of the trail can sport high grass, so you may need to wear long pants when hiking it.

Other Bayfield Trails

■ **Big Ravine Trails** – The in-city trail heads for a 2-mile round trip along a steep ravine lined with old-growth hemlocks. You'll find the trailhead at the Sweeney Avenue baseball field behind the out-field fence.

■ **Big Sand Bay Walking trails** – Paths cut across pine barrens on the Bayfield Peninsula northwest of town. The trails are on the west side of Old County Highway K Road, about 1.5 miles north of the Wis. Hwy. 13 junction.

■ **Iron Bridge Nature Hiking Trail** – Also known as the Gil Larsen Trail, the 0.75-mile trail follows a ravine creek under an old iron bridge to an over-look. Pick up the trail in Bayfield on Washington Avenue uphill from the ferry boat landing.

■ **Mt. Ashwabay Ski Area Hiking trails** – Several ski trails in winter turn to day hiking trails of varying lengths in summer. The ski area is located on Ski Hill Road south of Bayfield.

■ **Pike's Creek Hiking Trail** – The 2-mile round trip trail heads along Pike's Creek and past the state fish hatchery, which boasts two large ponds.

Fish species native to Lake Superior are raised there.

■ **Sioux River Flats Beach Trail** – For a great beach walk, try this 1.9-mile stretch south of Bayfield. From Wis. Hwy. 13, take Bayview Park Road to a parking area and follow the beach to the Sioux River.

Madeline Island

Ironically, the main reason some people visit Bayfield County is to leave it – that's because the village of Bayfield offers ferry service to Madeline Island, by far the most popular attraction among those traveling this far north...yet Madeline Island actually is part of Ashland County. But that's a trivial matter to most travelers, as Bayfield and Madeline Island are intimately connected in most people's minds.

Though Madeline Island is the largest of the famous 22 Apostle Islands it is not part of the national lakeshore. Madeline's crown jewel is Bay View State Park.

Bay View Trail, Boardwalk, nature trail
Big Bay State Park

Incredible views of Lake Superior await hikers traveling to Big Bay State Park.

Taking the Bay View Trail along with a boardwalk and a self-guided interpretive trail affords hikers a 5-mile round trip, though this can be cut in half if turning around at the boardwalk.

To avoid the Northwoods cold, visit in June and July. You'll have to first load your vehicle aboard the Madeline Island Ferry, which runs every half hour from Bayfield on the mainland to La Pointe on the island. After a 20-minute ride across the lake, take County Road H east for about four miles. Turn right/east on Hagen Road. The park entrance is in 2 miles; you'll need to pay an entry fee.

Continue on the park entry road (aka Haines Road), turning right onto Wilderness Road. Where the road loops is a parking lot. The trailhead is on the lot's east side.

An easy, well-maintained trail, you'll pass Point Picnic Area to the edge of Madeline Island. At one time, the island – as well as the other Apostle Islands – was part of the mainland. Four sets of glaciers during the past 100,000 years and the ensuing lakes have eroded the 600 million-year-old sedimentary rock and formed the islands.

At the tee intersection with Lake Superior before you, go left onto Bay View Trail (to the right is Point Trail). The wooded trail hugs the shoreline. You're certain to spot wildlife and likely will see some bluff caves. If staying overnight, do the trail at sunset – you won't be disappointed by the spectacular views over Lake Superior's Big Bay.

The largest of the Great Lakes sits atop hard basalt that formed 1.1 billion years ago when the North American continent literally was splitting.

Eventually this separation stopped, and the rift filled with sediment. Glaciers during the last Ice Age excavated these deposits and left the cold water that forms the lake.

As rounding the shoreline, Bay View Trail turns into Lagoon Ridge Trail; follow this for a few yards to the boardwalk. If short on time or if tired, you may want to turn back here. If the day is young and you're full of energy, go right, continuing along the boardwalk, which cuts through a white and red pine forest sitting upon Big Bay Sand Spit. Bearberry and wintergreen grows beneath the pines.

Nicely flat, the half-mile boardwalk offers benches for resting, interpretive signs, and more impressive lake views. A lagoon sits to the boardwalk's left.

Some 15,000 years ago when Madeline Island reappeared as the glaciers retreated and melted, the lagoon didn't exist and was part of Big Bay. Since then, wave action and lake currents built a pair of barrier beaches, creating the lagoon.

The boardwalk turns into the self-guided nature trail that runs up the spit. You may want to take a break along the beach for a swim.

The nature trail includes a couple of small loops in it. Watch for bald eagles that nest and raise their younglings in the park. Upon reaching the trail's end, turn around and return the way you came.

Before coming to the island, make sure you bring insect repellent. Bugs can be bothersome in the

trail's forested sections, and repellent sometimes can be difficult to find on the island.

Other Madeline Island Trails

■ **Big Bay Town Park Trail** – The trail heads east from the park entry road to a bridge that connects with a sand spit and beach along Big Bay. The beach trail can be followed south for about 0.2 miles to Big Bay State Park and then extended by connecting with the aforementioned Boardwalk Trail.

■ **Capser Trail** – The 2-mile one-way trail runs between a parking area on Middle Road/Chebomnicon Road and County Road H/Big Bay Road in the Madeline Island Wilderness Preserve as part of the Madeline Island Ski & Hiking Trail South Section. A stem trail leads to an observation deck overlooking a wetlands.

■ **Lagoon Ridge Trail** – The 2.6-mile round trip trail heads from Lake Superior around a lagoon to a campsite on Big Bay State Park's northern side. A good portion of it runs atop a ridge overlooking the lagoon and the Great Lake.

■ **North End Trail** – Logging roads and old survey lines have been reclaimed as a trail that with its side loop runs up to 7 miles long in the Madeline Island Wilderness Preserve. Three trailheads access the collection of loops and stems that also are collectively known as the Madeline Island Ski & Hiking Trail North Section.

■ **Nucy Meech Trail** – The Capser Trail can be extended 0.85 miles by taking this narrow path in the Madeline Island Wilderness Preserve's southern unit. It's being used to monitor the spread of buckthorn, barberry and other invasive species on the island.

■ **Point Trail and Point Trail Loop** – Point Trail and a portion of the Point Trail Loop skirt the Lake Superior shoreline with a beach area for a 1.7-mile hike in Big Bay State Park. Access the trail from the parking lot for the Point Picnic Area.

Apostle Island National Lakeshore

The picturesque Apostle Island National Lakeshore includes 21 of the 22 Apostle Islands and a stretch of shore on the Bayfield Peninsula. Other than the peninsula unit, you won't be able to reach any of the islands in the national lakeshore by vehicle – but you can sail there yourself or take any one of a number of charters from the nearby towns of Bayfield and Ashland.

Isolation from vehicular traffic makes each island a quiet and secluded paradise of Northwoods wilderness. Almost all of the islands contain hiking trails to enjoy. Among the most popular are trails are found on Michigan and Stockton islands, as well as the Bayfield Peninsula.

Lakeshore Mainland Trail

You don't have to leave the mainland to experience the beauty of the famous Apostle Islands National Lakeshore. A fairly new route, the Lakeshore Trail, runs through a Lake Superior forest, over an impressive sandstone cave formation, and along a windswept beach.

To reach Lakeshore Trail, take Wis. Hwy. 13 north from Bayfield. At Park Road, turn toward Meyers Beach. A large paved parking lot sits 0.4 miles away at the road's end.

Look for trail signs on the parking lot's northeast side. You'll head east through aspen, birch, several maple varieties, and a few pines. Given the mix of trees and their different fall leaf colors, early September is an ideal time for the hike; mosquitoes also will be few at that time of the year.

A few hundred yards from the parking lot, the trail goes up and down a gully, which in spring and early summer can boast running water. Stepping stones make for an easy fording, though.

When you cross a sand road, you're about 0.8 miles along the trial. Continue that same distance again, and you'll glimpse the lake and the trail's highlight: the Mawikwe Bay Sea Caves.

The lakes' crashing waves and millennia of winter ice carved out honeycombed caves and a 50-foot chasm that runs more than 200 feet long. A natural bridge runs over the formation. The tinted sandstone and rainbows from the spray gives the formation a magical feel.

The caves can't be accessed from the trail except during winter when the lake freezes (You may see kayakers at other times of the year clambering about the caves, however.). During winter, icicles hanging from the sandstone roofs appear otherworldly.

The trail skirts the chasm. If children are with you, make sure they stay away from the cliff edges and off the natural bridge. All are unstable due to constant erosion.

This marks a good place to turn back for a round-trip hike that is slightly more than three miles long. For a more ambitious hike, however, continue onward. After more than a mile on the bluff overlooking the sea caves, follow the trail inland through the forest. The flat trail winds through more hardwoods in a very peaceful setting.

Be forewarned that once in the forest, the trail can be difficult to follow. Fortunately, it soon meets a dirt road. Turn left onto the road, which drops about 80 feet in elevation, until reaching a sandy beach.

Seagulls are numerous here. The clump of trees across the lake's horizon is Eagle Island. Keep walking east and north along the shoreline for about a half mile or once it turns to cobble. Return the way you came for a roughly 10-mile round trip.

Though the trail is managed by the National Park Service, there is no fee for hikers to enter or park.

Michigan Island Trail

The easternmost Apostle Islands is Michigan Island. The 1.6-mile (round trip) Michigan Island Trail runs across it.

To reach the island, you'll need to take a private

boat. The dock for the island sits at the base of the bluff for the Michigan Island lighthouse on the island's southeast corner. Ascend the 142 steps to the lighthouse; gear and supplies can be pulled up on a cable car using a winch.

A lighthouse has been on the island since 1856 – but only because of a mix-up. The structure was to have been built on nearby Long Island, but a last minute change by a field rep caused its location to be moved to Michigan Island.

One of six historic lighthouses in the Apostle Islands, the Michigan Island site underwent some moderate repairs in late 2012. The public now can access the lighthouse and see exhibits related to it; park volunteers usually offer tours in late morning and early afternoon.

Next to the historical lighthouse is a cylindrical steel tower that replaced its predecessor. Originally located on the Delaware River, the tower was brought to Wisconsin. It's now the state's tallest lighthouse.

From the bluff tops looking southwest, you'll see Madeline Island in the distance. The trailhead begins on an unmarked path behind the lighthouse keeper's home, winding into a second growth woods away from Lake Superior's open waters. The trail runs northwest down glacial till through some low-lying and even marshy areas.

In a quarter mile, you'll reach a beach on the island's western shore. In the distance is Presque

Isle Point, which is part of neighboring Stockton Island.

Turn left/southwest for a walk along the beach, where driftwood and shells are ubiquitous. A marsh sits inland, separated from the beach by brush. Blue herons frequent the marsh.

After 0.55 miles, the beach reaches a primitive campsite on a sandspit sitting at the island's southwest end. Fires are allowed at the site, and boats can be moored there.

If feeling adventurous, extend the hike by taking the beach as it curves along the island's southern shore. The remains of an old fishing camp with a broken boat are in 0.4 miles. Heavy brush and storm-tossed tree trunks makes the beach a difficult walk back to the lighthouses, however, so rather than making a loop consider returning on the route that you came.

Definitely bring insect repellent if hiking in summer. Also be aware that Lake Superior's storms can leave you stranded on the island for two or three days at a time, so if camping carry enough supplies.

Other National Lakeshore Trails

To reach any island in the national lakeshore, you'll need to take a boat or waterplane. A variety of charters are available in Bayfield, Ashland and on Madeline Island. Some great trails to explore on these remote islands include:

■ **Anderson Point Trail** – Stockton Island sits northeast of Hermit Island, directly north of Madeline and northwest of Michigan islands. A popular summer destination, Stockton Island boasts 14 miles of maintained day hiking trails. This 1.4-mile trail heads south of the dock through a forest of old growth hemlocks that parallels the point's rocky shoreline. It ends at the Julian Bay beach, where you'll want to take off your shoes as the sand "sings" when walked upon. To make it a loop, take the Julian Bay Trail back to the docks for a 1.8-mile walk.

■ **Basswood Island Loop** – From the mainland, the closest Apostle Island that's part of the national lakeshore is Basswood Island. The island sits between Bayfield Peninsula to the west and Madeline Island to the south and east. A lone trail runs on the island's southern end. A 5.4-mile loop, the trailhead is on a clearing up the hill from the island's dock along its western shore.

■ **Loop Trail** – Oak Island sits roughly in the middle of the national lakeshore and offers 11.5 miles of day hiking trails. It also boasts the national lakeshore's highest elevation at 1081 feet above sea level. The Oak Island dock leaves you at Campsite B and the trailhead for this 5.2-mile trail, which heads along the shore and through woods.

Washburn

Bayfield County's largest city, Washburn offers travelers access to Chequamegon Bay and is a short distance from a number of public lands. Among them is the Chequamegon National Forest and its Mt. Valhalla trails, the recently created Houghton Falls Nature Preserve, and Big Rock County Park. Hiking trails can be found in each of these areas.

Houghton Falls Trail
Houghton Falls Nature Preserve

Day hikers can walk across an ancient riverbed and see fascinating rock formations north of Washburn at the Houghton Falls Nature Preserve.

The 1.34-mile round trip trail is packed dirt and fairly flat. Because it follows a stream, it can be muddy following rainfalls.

To reach the trail, from Washburn take Wis. Hwy. 13 north. Turn right/east onto Houghton Falls Road. In a half-mile, the road reaches the Houghton Falls Nature Preserve parking lot on the right/south.

The trail heads roughly south for about a quarter mile through a thick forest of majestic, old growth white and red pine.

It then comes to an ancient riverbed known as Echo Dells, where an intermittent stream that flows southeast for about 0.4 miles to Lake Superior.

Wind and water have smoothed and rounded the dells' pink sandstone canyon walls. Pools at the stream's deepest points, small caves, and cascades line the gorge. The sandstone, set down a billion years ago in the pre-Cambrian era, offers cathedral-like acoustics.

At spots, tall and thick trees have fallen across the canyon's rim. The walls are high enough that hikers can walk beneath the massive trunks.

Old growth hemlock as well as yellow birch and mountain maple form the gorge's canopy. Hemlock rarely grows much farther west than Wisconsin.

Between the shade and stream, the understory remains lush with various ferns, small enchanter's nightshade, thimbleberry, and wood sorrel. In mid-August, watch for blooming Indian Pipe; a plethora of mushrooms also are present.

As the trail turns southwest, look up at the canyon rim, where you may be lucky enough to spot white-tailed deer. The cliff shelves support Canada yew, one of the deer's favorite shrubs.

Once the narrow but well-marked path reaches Lake Superior, you'll stand atop weather-sculpted cliffs on the southern portion of Houghton Point. About 15 feet above Chequamegon Bay, the overlook provides great views of the Apostle Islands.

Also keep an eye out for a variety of resident and migratory birds. The rocky shoreline is home to bald eagle, Canada warbler, least flycatcher, merlin, veery, and wood thrush.

Inset from the point, Houghton Falls drops into a rippled sandy cove. The falls are best seen during spring. They're typically just a trickle during late summer and autumn, but the tradeoff is few if any mosquitoes at that time of the year.

Another fun highlight of the trail, especially for kids, is a 25-foot arched wooden bridge crossing the creek.

The preserve is 76-acres in size and lacks facilities. Sometimes maps refer to it as the "Houghton Falls State Natural Area" or the "Houghton Falls Natural Area."

Teuton Trail Loop C
Chequamegon National Forest

Day hikers during summer can enjoy a set of trails that the U.S. Olympic Nordic Ski Team once trained on near Washburn.

A pair of three loops – the Teuton and the Valkyrie – make up the Mt. Valhalla trails in the Chequamegon National Forest. A shortened version of the Teuton Trail System's Loop C makes for a somewhat challenging 2.75-mile hike.

To reach the trail, from Washburn take County Road C north for 8.5 miles. The parking lot is on the road's south side, where the Teuton Trails are located (The Valkyrie Trails are on the north.); you'll need a pass to park your vehicle in the national forest.

From the parking lot, follow the trail clockwise (the opposite way skiers take it), by heading south past the shelter. Upon reaching the split in the trail, go left/southeast, putting you on Loop C.

From there, you'll begin traveling along the side of Mt. Valhalla and soon cross Four Mile Creek. The trail ultimately climbs about 170 feet in elevation with few level areas.

You may be too busy taking in Mt. Valhalla's natural beauty to notice. The trail runs through a Northern hardwood forest – rare for the Bayfield Peninsula – full of big tooth aspen, black oak, pa-per birch, and sugar maple trees, with a few scat-tered Eastern white pines. Ferns blanket the forest floor.

After a quarter mile, the trail curves south then west. You'll soon parallel Four Mile Creek and then cross it again. A variety of frogs, chipmunks and red squirrels inhabit this area, and you're likely to hear if not see them on the trail.

In another mile, the trail curves north. Keep an ear out for the many songbirds in the forest, including the yellow-bellied sapsucker, blue jays, wood thrush, robins, warblers, sparrows and grosbeaks.

After about a quarter mile when you come to a trail junction, go right/east. You'r e now on Loop B.

As the trail turns sharp to the north, you'll come the closest to reaching Mt. Valhalla's summit. The mountain tops out at 1388 feet, and you'll be about 110 feet below it.

Though technically not a mountain, Mt. Valhalla appears high given the Bayfield Peninsula's fairly low elevation. But it's not even the highest point in the county; the tallest is Mt. Telemark at 1700 feet.

Loop B meanders downhill in a northerly direction for about 0.75 miles. The trail then makes a hard right for 0.5 miles with Loop A joining it along the way. This will take you back to the parking lot.

Don't worry about getting confused by all of the trail junctions and intersecting snowmobile trails that cross your route. All of the Teuton's trails are well-signed, and a metal map is at every junction.

Other Washburn Trails

■ **Big Rock County Park trails** – Trails ramble through the park, split in half by a first-class steelhead trout stream, the Sioux River. Wildlife sightings are a certainty for hikers.

■ **Birch Grove Campground Trail** – Located at the Birch Grove Campground in the Chequamegon National Forest, the trail circles East Twin Lake for a 1-mile loop. Trailheads are located at both boat landings.

■ **Henkens Road Walking trails** – Two trails can be found off Henkins Road about 1.5 miles from the Star Route Road intersection northwest of Washburn. A trailhead is located on each side of the road.

■ **Washburn Lakefront Parkway Walking Trail** – In Washburn, the 1.34-mile trail over an abandoned railroad grade runs along Lake Superior, passing three beaches, the picturesque marina, and several historical sites. The trail connects Thompson West End Park and Memorial Park.

■ **Washburn School Forest and Environmental Education Center trails** – Ski trails can be hiked during summer in this heavily wooded center. The forest is on Eighth Avenue West outside of Washburn.

Ashland

P art of the city of Ashland spills into Bayfield County, and often travelers on their way to Bayfield or Madeline Island pass through the town. It offers excellent access to Chequamegon Bay via an urban hiking trail and is a short distance from the Chequamegon National Forest. One end of the Tri-County Trail, a former railroad bed converted to hiking trail that runs through Bayfield County to Superior, starts in Ashland. The city's highlight in Bayfield County is the Northern Great Lakes Visitor Center, which offers exhibits, demonstrations, and a trail, all dedicated to fostering an understanding of Lake Superior's natural history and man's interaction with the largest of the Great Lakes.

Interpretive Boardwalk Trail
Northern Great Lakes Visitor Center

Day hikers can wander along a trail that wends its way through three coastal wetland ecosystems: a sedge meadow, a black ash swamp, and a cedar and tamarack swamp near Ashland.

The Interpretive Boardwalk Trail runs 0.75-miles

at the Northern Great Lakes Visitor Center west of town.

To reach the trail, from Ashland take U.S. Hwy. 2 west. Turn right/west onto County Road G. The visitor center is the next right/left. Park in the center's lot.

On the lot's north side, take the paved trail heading northwest. After about 30 yards of lawn, the trail enters a sedge meadow and turns into a boardwalk.

Sedges – which look like tall grass – rushes and forbs dominate the sedge meadow. Those plants flourish on the wetland's saturated soils.

Thanks to the sedge meadow and the center sitting next to the Whittlesey Creek National Wildlife Refuge, the trail offers a number of birdwatching opportunities. Among the highlights are bald eagles, migratory raptors, and spring warblers.

As the trail reaches the northern edge of its loop, it leaves the sedge meadow for the wooded swamp ecosystems.

The black ash swamp, so named for the tree that dominates that wetlands, also is known as a northern hardwood swamp. It typically occurs alongside lakes or streams. Because the landscape drains poorly, often the soil is a mucky sand.

A cedar and tamarack swamp, sometimes called a coniferous swamp, is named for the northern white cedar and tamarack that rule this type of wetlands. A foot of water can inundate it. When the flood recedes, ferns often grow in the understory.

As veering southeast, the trail runs along the border of the sedge meadow and the wooded swamps. At the first intersection in that transition area, continue straight/southeast.

Upon reaching the lawn area at the loop's end, the trail becomes paved again. Turn left/south to re-enter the parking lot.

If you have children, be sure to stop at the visitor center, where they can crawl through a beaver lodge and engage in other fun (but educational!) activities. Admission is free.

As you're entering wetlands, don and carry bug spray on the hike. The trail is handicap accessible.

Other Ashland Trails

■ **Tri-County Corridor Trail segment** – On its way to Superior, the trail runs west out of town. A pastoral segment is between Pine Creek Road and County Road G. Park at the Moquah Town Hall and head east for a 1-mile round trip.

■ **Waterfront Trail** – This 10-mile trail loops around the city of Ashland, passing through several parks and a beach along the way. A scenic segment runs along the Lake Superior shoreline from Maslowski Beach to Howard Pearson Plaza for about 2 miles one-way.

■ Also see *Ashland County* below.

Drummond

Entirely surrounded by the Chequamegon National Forest, the village of Drummond is a popular destination for campers, hikers, skiers, and fishermen. Well over two dozen lakes, most notably Lake Owen, can be found within 10 miles of town. Among the premier hiking routes near the village is the North Country National Scenic Trail, which stretches from New York state to North Dakota.

Drummond Woods Interpretative Trail
Chequamegon National Forest

Massive trees from an old growth forest and vibrant autumn colors await day hikers on the Drummond Woods Trail in the Chequamegon National Forest.

The 0.75-mile trail runs through the Drummond Woods, where a number of trees survived the 1800s lumberjacking of the Wisconsin Northwoods. The route sometimes is referred to on maps and in literature as the "Drummond Woods Trail."

To reach the trailhead, from Drummond, take U.S. Hwy. 63 north. In one mile, turn left/west onto Old 63 N (aka Forest Road 235). About 150 feet from that intersection on the right is a small pull-off for parking.

From the lot, take the stem trail northwest into the Drummond Woods. Coming to the loop, go left/west or clockwise. The loop is flat and fairly easy for children.

Heading through a northern hardwood forest, the trail marks an excellent spot to enjoy fall colors: the yellows of basswood and birch; the oranges of sugar maples; and the scarlet of black ash and red maple. Evergreens dominate the canopy with towering white and red pines and hemlocks.

The hemlocks are particularly impressive. Some of them measure 40 inches around.

The ground cover also offers a show, especially in spring. Violets, trillium and humble bellwort grow amid princess pine. When reaching wetter areas, blue flag iris flourishes in clumps.

A little more than halfway through the hike, the trail runs alongside a tamarack-black spruce swamp. On the ground, look for Labrador tea, leatherleaf, and pink lady slippers. One other surprise is the carnivorous pitcher plant, which traps insects in its blossom and then digests them.

Along the loop's north side, you can extend the hike by taking the intersecting North Country Trail a ways into the backcountry.

If visiting the region during winter, the trail is popular among snowshoers.

Lake Owen Loop
North Country National Scenic Trail

Visitors to Drummond can hike a segment of the 4,600-mile North Country National Scenic Trail in an enjoyable route I've christened the "Lake Owen Loop."

The North Country trail stretches from North Dakota to New York, cutting through four Wisconsin counties along the way. The Badger state boasts the highest percentage of completed and the longest continuous stretch of the trail in the country. In Bayfield County, the trail cuts through the popular Chequamegon National Forest.

About five miles long, the Lake Owen Loop is best done in autumn when the bug count is down and the trees are ablaze with color. Early spring is good for avoiding mosquitoes but may force you to cross two intermittent streams flush that time of year with snowmelt.

To reach the trail, from U.S. Hwy. 63 in Drummond, take North Lake Owen Drive (aka Forest Road 213) south. You'll pass Roger Lake. When you come to Lake Owen, look for the intersection with Forest Road 216 (aka as Lake Owen Station Road). Stay on FR 213 and round the northern tip of Lake Owen. Turn right into the picnic grounds, where you'll park. A swimming beach also is on site.

From the picnic area, look east and pick up the trail where it intersects the forest road. The North Country trail is fairly flat with elevation shifting about 50 feet during the hike.

Walk south, cutting between the northern tip of Lake Owen and a 35-foot deep pond. An intermittent stream connects it to the lake.

The trail follows the north shore of Lake Owen, forming a U. Mixed hardwoods and pines line the lake. Hemlock, oak, maple and white pine often tower over the dirt path.

As reaching the bottom of the U's western side, you'll cross a road. You're unlikely to see many people, though, as this side of Lake Owen is little used compared to its other shorelines, which sport camps and boat ramps.

At 1,323 acres with a maximum depth of 95 feet, Lake Owen boasts very clear water, making it an ideal habitat for largemouth and smallmouth bass, muskie, Northern pike, walleye and panfish.

About midway at the U's bottom, there's a second intermittent stream to cross. You'll then spot Twin Lakes Campgrounds on the opposite shore.

As coming up the U's eastern side, the trail veers away from lake. Watch for the wildlife that makes this area home. White-tailed deer, squirrels, chipmunks and frogs are certain to be seen, but also keep an eye out for other animals' tracks, especially those of raccoons. Keep your ears peeled for the call of loons, which nest on the area's lakes.

After crossing a forest road, you'll walk past a pond to the right and then one to the left. Finally, you'll head past yet another pond, this one up to 14 feet deep, on the right.

Rejoining Forest Road 213, you can walk alongside it back to your vehicle. On the way you will first pass Forest Road 217, aka Cutacross Road, which goes north, and then Horseshoe Road, which goes south.

Upon reaching your start point, end the day with a picnic and swim.

Other Drummond Trails

■ **Anderson Grade trail in Rainbow Lake Wilderness Area** – The 4-mile trail crosses the Rainbow Lake Wilderness Area from east to west over rolling terrain. Balsam fir, Northern hardwoods, paper birch and pines line the trail.

■ **Antler Trail** – Six trails make up the Drummond Ski Trail system southeast of town. This 2-mile route heads over gentle terrain through a Northern hardwood forest.

■ **Porcupine Lake Wilderness Trail** – Over a mix of rolling hills and fairly flat terrain, the trail cuts through a forest of hemlock, maple, oak and white pine. Expect to see white-tailed deer, loons, and songbirds galore, as well as signs of bear, coyote and fox.

■ **Rainbow Lake Wilderness Area trails** – Six miles of the trail crosses the wilderness area from northwest to southwest. Built on an old narrow gauge logging bed, it passes four lakes.

■ **Two Lakes Campground Trail** – A 1.5-mile trail loops around Bass Lake near the campground in the national forest. Northern hardwoods and pines tower over the trail.

Cable

A gateway to Bayfield County, many travelers make the village their destination as well, and for good reason. The Chequamegon National Forest stretches to the north and east while the St. Croix National Scenic Riverway heads to the southwest into Saywer and Washburn counties. Among the village's highlights is the Birkebeiner Trail; while mainly used for skiing, it also can be hiked during other seasons.

Birkebeiner Trail

Though known primarily for the annual ski race held on it, Wisconsin's massive Birkebeiner Trail system also makes a great hiking route in summer.

With more than 66 miles of trails, all maintained by the nonprofit American Birkebeiner Ski Foundation, "The Birkie Trail," as its fans affectionately call it, offers multiple trailheads, loops and variations between Cable and Hayward. One segment that's easy to locate and hike is the Birkie's opening section, a 2.6-mile round trip when treated as an out-and-back trail.

To reach the trailhead, in Cable from County Road

M go south onto Randysek Road. After crossing the Namekagon River, turn left/east onto McNaught Road. Drive about 1.7 miles then park to the side of one of the mowed paths on the road's left/north side.

After walking through the treeline, the Cable Union Airport comes into the view. The trail heads west from the airport.

Built for bicycling and cross-country skiing races, Birkie Ridge is wide and void of roots and stones.

The entire opening segment of the trail runs through a classic Northern hardwoods forest of sugar maple, basswood, beech, white ash, and yellow birch, making for a colorful autumn walk. Hemlock and fir also appear in the mix.

The opening segment sits inside the St. Croix National Scenic Riverway. The Namekagon River, protected by the National Park Service unit, flows north of the trail on its way to Hayward.

The entire Birkie trail system is a 40-plus year project in the making. The first cross-country ski race was held on it in 1973; today, it's the largest race of its kind in North America, attracting about 10,000 participants and 15,000 spectators.

Northwoods promoter Tony Wise is largely credited with starting the race and helping to popularize modern-day cross-country skiing. In 1972, he built cross-country trails at his Telemark Ski Area near Cable then a year later started the Birkie race.

The Birkie trail system gets its name from Norway's Birkebeinerrennet cross-country event, which commemorates when skiers in 1206 AD smuggled the king's illegitimate son to safety during a civil war. The skiers were soldiers in the Birkebiener Party.

Upon reaching a power line, the trail veers southeast and crosses McNaught Road. The power line marks a good point to turn back.

Be aware that mountain bikers and joggers also use the Birkie. There's plenty of space for both, but on race days the trail system will be closed to hikers; check *www.birkie.com/trail* to see when events are planned.

Forest Lodge Nature Trail
Chequamegon National Forest

Among the best hikes to learn about the Wisconsin northwoods is the Forest Lodge Nature Trail, east of Cable. Located in the Chequamegon National Forest, the 1.5-mile loop is maintained in cooperation with the Cable Natural History Museum.

Any dry summer day is excellent for hiking the trail, and fall colors are spectacular with trees usually remaining golden until the third week in October.

To reach the trail, take County Road M for about 8.6 miles east of Cable. Turn left/north on Garmish Road. The parking lot/trailhead is a mile later on the road's right/south side. A forest pass is required to park.

From the lot, head straight south into an old field. If you turn left, you'll end up on the neighboring Conservancy Trail.

While fairly flat, the trail does narrow from four- to two-feet wide upon reaching the woods. The forested section of the trail sports some rough tread as well.

The trail rambles through a number of ecosystems, offering a mini-walk through the region's natural history.

Among the ecosystems is a lowland bog, surrounded by spruce and slender-stemmed cotton grass. Here you'll also find the carnivorous bog-dwelling pitcher plant.

Another ecosystem – now rare for northern Wisconsin – is of old-growth white pines. During the 1880s when pioneers settled the area, the white pine dominated; after being logged off, hardwoods replaced them.

A good portion of the trail is that newer upland hardwood forest. Chipmunks are abundant there.

One element of the landscape hasn't changed, though: glacial erratics. These are boulders and rocks brought here during the last ice age that are different in color and composition than those "native" to the area.

Hikers also will walk through a grove of hemlocks, which looks like a scene out of a fairy tale, and an experimental prairie.

An excellent way to identify and learn more about these sights is the interpretive booklet available at the Cable Natural History Museum, located in Cable at 13470 County Road M.

Forest Road 1919B/BA Trail
Chequamegon National Forest

Day hikers can walk through the area where Wisconsin's first Thanksgiving took place just a few decades after the Pilgrims held the very first one at Plymouth Plantation.

The unnamed trail – which I've christened the Forest Road 1919B/BA Trail because of the jeep trails it follows in the Chequamegon National Forest – takes hikers on a 1.14-mile round trip to the headwaters of the Chippewa River. Near that waterway in what is now the southeastern corner of Bayfield County, local Native Americans rescued three starving French explorers by providing a feast in a story with remarkable parallels to the Pilgrims' harvest banquet.

To reach the trailhead, from Cable take County Road M east. Before arriving in Clam Lake, turn left/north onto Forest Road 191 (aka as Taylor Lake Road and Old Grade Road). Then turn left/southwest onto Forest Road 1919 (aka Job Corps Road). Follow this to its terminus at Chippewa Lake, parking off the road.

A narrow trail heads to a campsite on the shores of Chippewa Lake. Though expansive at 280 acres, the lake is fairly shallow at only 11 feet. From it rises the West Fork Chippewa River.

It was near the lake in late 1658 that French explorers Pierre Esprit Radisson and Médard Chouart Sieur des Groseilliers ran out of food during a particularly harsh winter.

To survive, they ate their dogs then retraced their steps to former camps so they could dig the refuse of their previous meals from snowbanks for food. Then they crushed bones into powder and boiled guts and skin for sustenance. Finally, they ate wood. "...the rest goes downe our throats, eating heartily these things most abhorred," Radisson wrote.

From the lakeshore, walk back to Forest Road 1919 and turn right/south onto Forest Road 1919B. The trail heads through a Northern hardwood forest, a beautiful hike in autumn when gold, orange and crimson leaves dominate the skyline.

In 1659, a group of Odowa (Ottowa) Indians came across the two explorers. The Odowa gave them new clothes and most importantly provided a banquet of wild turkey and rice as well as other fowl. Groseilliers gave "a speech of thanksgiving."

Where the trail splits, go left onto Forest Road 1919BA. This heads to the edge of the West Fork Chippewa River. The bulk of the hike is on FR 19191BA.

Upon reaching the river, to the northwest are marshlands surrounding Chippewa Lake. Downstream, the fork meanders before joining with the East Fork Chippewa River and forming the Chippewa River proper, which flows for 130 miles into the Mississippi River.

Just as the Wampanoags had saved the Pilgrims from starvation by showing them how to raise crops such as corn and squash, so the Odowa similarly saved the French explorers from certain death by the sharing of food. With that gesture, Radisson and Groseilliers were able to return to their base in eastern Canada. The Wisconsin Historical Society considers it the state's first Thanksgiving celebration involving Europeans and Native Americans.

From the West Fork Chippewa River's shoreline, return the way you came to your vehicle.

Namekagon Dam Landing Trail
St. Croix National Scenic Riverway

Day hikers can walk along the the Namekagon River's headwaters on a trail in the easternmost tip of the St. Croix National Scenic Riverway.

The 1.3-mile round trip walk is located in the southwest corner of the Chequamegon National Forest. June through September mark the best months to hike the trail.

To reach the trailhead, from Cable, take County

Road M east. In about eight miles and after entering the national forest, turn left/north onto Dam Road/Forest Road 211. After crossing the Namekagon, take the first right, which heads to a small dam. A parking lot is located there.

The dam backs up the river into a flowage that heads east to Lake Namakagon (Note the different spelling from the river). The 2897-acre glacial lake in southern Bayfield County boasts 43.67 miles of shoreline. One of only three managed trophy muskie lakes in Wisconsin, it reaches a depth of 38 feet and even has islands.

From the dam, hike back up to Dam Road, go left, and walk alongside the asphalt back across the bridge. The bridge's corner offers a great view of the dam to the east and the narrow river to the west, which runs for 101 miles to the St. Croix River.

Continue walking south on Dam Road. In about a thousand feet from the bridge, turn right/northwest onto Forest Road 1730. The jeep trail follows the top of the bluff overlooking the Namekagon. The bluff line runs anywhere from 20 to 40 feet higher than the river, which sits at a fairly even 1400 feet above sea level.

The trail sits beneath a canopy of mixed Northern hardwoods. During autumn, it makes for a fantastic display of golds and oranges accented with reds and dark evergreens.

The river below, nestled in a fen forest, is popular

with canoeists and kayakers during summer. A series of small rapids can be found about two miles below the dam; after the rapids, the river widens, and the fen forest gives way to open marsh.

On the bluff line trail, in about 350 feet from Dam Road, you'll cross a creek that flows into the Namekagon. Watch for beaver, which create ponds out of the stream and wetlands. Sometimes on the main river, beaver dams even will stop the paddlers.

In about 1000 feet from the creek, the trail ends at a high point of 1439 feet. From there, head back the way you came.

During early to mid-summer, be sure to carry insect repellant. Also, note that official maps do not call this the Namekagon Dam Landing Trail; the name is a convention for this book.

Other Cable Trails

■ **Namekagon Trail East Loop** – Located northeast of town in the Chequamegon National Forest, the 1-mile East Loop of this three-loop trail can be hiked in summer. You're very likely to hear and possibly even spot Northwoods wildlife along the walk.

■ **North End Trail** – South of town, this ski trail in winter is often day hiked the other seasons. Consisting of several crisscrossing routes, combine the Ridge and Bear Paw loops for a 1.6-mile walk.

■ **Rock Lake Trail** – Narrow loops of varying lengths run through the Chequamegon around

Rock, Frels and Hildebrand lakes. Hiking is best on the segments running from Forest Road 207 to any of these lakes.

Iron River

The western gateway to Bayfield County, Iron River is a popular destination for many who love the outdoors. It is located about halfway between the Brule River State Forest to the west and the Chequamegon National Forest to the east. The Tri-County Cooridor Trail runs through town between Superior and Ashland while the North County National Scenic Trail passes nearby.

Erick Lake segment
North Country National Scenic Trail

Day hikers can walk a segment of what is considered one of the nation's premier trails.

The Erick Lake segment of the North Country National Scenic Trail heads along a ridgeline through a new growth forest. It runs 4 miles one-way.

To reach the trail, from Iron River head south on County Road A. South of the second intersection with Bradfield Road, park in the lot on County Road A's southeast side. The North Country Trail heads northwest and southeast from the lot. Go left/northwest from the lot and cross County Road A.

Running 4600 miles from New York state to North Dakota, when completed the North Country Trail will be twice the length of the Appalachian Trail and the longest hiking trail in the United States. About 61 miles of the North Country Trail crosses Bayfield County.

At 0.12 miles from the trailhead, the Erick Lake Segment gains elevation, climbing to one of the higher points along the trail, a hill at 1286 feet above sea level. From there, the dirt path generally follows a ridgeline as heading through woods and pine barrens.

Though the National Park Service studied the concept of a North Country Trail during the late 1960s, not until 1980 did Congress approve the route's creation. New segments are added almost every year; at one time, the parking lot on County Road A marked the trail's western terminus.

At about 1.9 miles from the trailhead, the route crosses Banana Belt Road. From there, the trail generally descends as heading toward the segment's namesake.

In another 1.9 miles, Erick Lake comes into view on the trail's north side. An 8-acre lake with a maximum depth of 26 feet, public campsites are nearby.

When the segment reaches Pero Road (aka Hughes Town Hall Road farther north), about 0.08 miles from the lake, turnaround. The complete hike runs 8-miles round trip.

Iron River National Fish Hatchery Trail

This day hiking trail north of Iron River offers the opportunity to learn about the life cycle of fish and the importance of national fish hatcheries.

Three miles of trails cut through 1,200 acres of the U.S. Fish and Wildlife Service's Iron River National Fish Hatchery facility. A 2.4-mile segment of those interpretive trails with a stop at the visitor center can make for a fun and educational day.

To reach the hatchery, take County Road A north from Iron River for 6.6 miles. Turn left/east on Fairview Road. The hatchery entrance is in one mile.

Park at the visitor center. Before hitting the trail, check in at the center.

For the trailhead, continue walking south on the road you drove in on. After about 0.2 miles, turn right onto a jeep trail heading southeast. The trail enters a wooded area.

The fish hatchery's location should come as no surprise. It's only a few miles from Lake Superior, as evidenced by the pine barrens on the Bayfield Peninsula that the trail passes through.

In 0.3 miles, take the trail south. After another 0.2 miles, the trail curves west.

The hatchery annually rears about 2 million trout that are then placed in Lake Superior, Lake Michigan, Lake Huron and some of their tributaries. Research also is conducted. It was established in 1979.

About 0.5 miles later, the trail reaches Weidenaar Road. To avoid walking alongside the highway, turn back there.

Upon returning to the parking lot, be sure to stop at the visitor center. Aquariums in the hatchery's Main Building and the early rearing tank-room also will be interesting to see, especially for children.

When at the hatchery, remind children with you to keep their hands out of the raceways. Doing so helps prevent disease from spreading among fish.

Other Iron River Trails

■ **Flag River Walking Trail** – North of Iron River on Flag Road a half-mile from Battle Axe Road, the trail meanders west near the Flag River. Groves of Northern hardwoods and evergreens shade the path.

■ **Long Lake Picnic Area Trail** – This 1.2-mile trail in the Chequamegon National Forest circles Long Lake and includes a boardwalk into a marsh. A picnic area is on the grounds; a parking fee is required.

■ **North Country National Scenic Trail, Brule River State Forest segment** – West of Iron River, a segment of this multi-state trails runs through the Brule River State Forest. From the parking lot off of Wis. Hwy. 27 near Radio Station Road, take the trail north for about two miles to Rush River Road; turn left onto Rush Road River, crossing Hwy. 27, for views of Big Lake.

■ **Ruth Lake Walking Trails** – On Ruth Lake Road, a half-mile from the County Road A intersection, trails begin on both sides of the highway. Go west to skirt the wooded southern end of Lake Ruth in the Chequamegon National Forest.

■ **Tomahawk Lake trails** – Off of Moore Road about 1.5 miles from the Island Lake Road intersection, walking paths run through wooded areas. Trails begin on either side of the road.

■ **Tri-County Corridor Trail, Wentzel Lake segment** – The trail connecting Superior and Ashland runs through Iron River. East of town, take the segment east from Topside Road east past Wentzel Lake and a pond to Forest Road 417 for a 3.8-mile one-way hike.

Cornucopia
and Red Cliff

Though views are scenic along Wis. Hwy. 13 that leads to and connects these villages, public facilities and hiking trails are sparse compared to the rest of the county. One major draw is the mainland unit of the Apostle Islands National Lakeshore, where the Mawikwe Bay Sea Caves can be accessed (For a description of that hiking route, see the previous entry for the **Lakeshore Mainland Trail** in the section about the Apostle Islands National Lakeshore).

Cornucopia

■ **Cornucopia Walking Trail** – This short trail runs along Lake Superior's south shore through the fishing village.

■ **Lost Creek Falls Walking Trail** – Located south of Cornucopia on the peninsula's west side, the trail heads for less than mile one way through pine barrens to Lost Creek. The trailhead is at the end of Trail Road off of County Road C.

■ **Spring Creek Walking Trails** – About 3.5 miles

miles south of Cornucopia on County Road C, a set of trails run through the pine barrens near the Siskiwit River and lakes. Look on the road's east side for the trailhead.

Red Cliff

■ **Raspberry River Walking Trail** – Northwest of Red Cliff, the trail heads through pine barrens to the Raspberry River, which ultimately flows into Lake Superior. The trailhead is at the intersection of Old County Highway K Road and Rowley Road.

Across the County Line

Bayfield County sits at the center of outdoors activity in the Wisconsin Northwoods. Three counties that are popular tourism destinations in their own right surround it. Ashland County is to the east and includes wide swaths of the Chequamegon National Forest as well as Copper Falls State Park. To the south is Sawyer County, which includes more of the Chequamegon, a stretch of the St. Croix National Scenic Riverway, and Flambeau River State Forest. To the west is Douglas County with the Brule River State Forest and the northern Wisconsin's largest city, Superior. Each of these counties offer a number of exceptional day hiking opportunities that easily can be reached from Bayfield County.

The county also shares a tangential border with Washburn County to the southwest; no direct routes quickly connect the two jurisdictions, however, so it is not included in this guidebook.

Ashland County

D ay hikers can enjoy a plethora of trails at three major outdoors attractions in Ashland County, which sits along Bayfield County's eastern border. Covering close to a quarter of the county's land area is the Chequamegon National Forest. To the forest's northeast is Copper Falls State Park, which offers a number of geologic wonders, including waterfalls. To the north are the Apostle Islands, which boasts beautiful Big Bay State Park on Madeline Island (see previous article) and a number of other trails in the Apostle Islands National Lakeshore (see previous article).

Morgan Falls St. Peter's Dome Trail
Chequamegon National Forest

An 80-foot waterfall and impressive vista with views 20 miles around await day hkers south of Ashland.

The Morgan Falls St. Peter's Dome Trail in the Chequamegon National Forest actually can be broken into two trails depending on your time and energy. The first 0.6 miles of the trail heads to Morgan Falls (for a 1.2-mile round trip), or you can continue another 1.2 miles to the top of St. Peter's Dome (for a 3.6-miles round trip).

Late spring to early fall is the best time to walk the trail.

To reach the trailhead, take U.S. Hwy. 63 about 22 miles north of Cable. Turn east onto County Road E, driving six miles to Ashland-Bayfield Road (aka Forest Road 199). Turn south. It's 4.2 miles to the parking lot. Watch for the trailhead sign at the parking lot.

Either a day pass or an annual forest pass is needed to travel to the trailhead (and is required throughout the Chequamegon).

The first portion of the trail is fairly flat and graveled and even accessible for people with disabilities. After a half-mile walk through a wooded area, Morgan Falls – Wisconsin's second highest waterfall – comes into view. The water zigzags some dozen feet down a rock face before splashing into a small pool. It overflows the pool falling another eight feet in different streams down a crooked granite cliff to the bottom in an intimate setting.

Be forewarned: During drought years, the water flow can be a little better than a trickle.

If continuing on to St. Peter's Dome, the trail gets a little more rugged, becoming a dirt path cutting over roots and stones across shallow creeks. The autumn colors are impressive, and in spring wildflowers including the large-flowered **trillium**, violets and Dutchman's-breeches dot the undergrowth and trail sides.

Other sights are located on the way. Among them is a circular stone cistern built at an abandoned Civilian Conservation Corps campground constructed during the 1930s.

A stone quarry from the mid-20th century (red granite is used to make counter-tops) also exists; it also is no longer in operation.

A number of rare ferns are situated along the trail. Among them are Braun's hollyfern, woodfern, and northern maidenhair fern. Hemlock and Canada yew also abound in large patches.

The trail does become steep as ascending St. Peter's Dome, which sits at 1,565 feet elevation.

From atop this ancient formation of red granite, Chequamagon Bay in Lake Superior at 20 miles away is visible on clear and dry days. With binoculars, you also might be able to spot the Michigan Island lighthouse, about 33 miles away, if you look northeast through a gap in the trees.

The vista is a massive red granite dome that began to form some 1.2 billion years ago. Magma crystallized underground, mixing with quartz and feldspar, which gives the granite a pink to orange coloring. Weathering over the eons has brought the granite "above" ground.

From the dome top, take the same route back to the trailhead.

Red Granite Falls Trail
Copper Falls State Park

A river rapids over billion-year-old red-tinged rock awaits day hikers on the Red Granite Falls Trail in Copper Falls State Park.

The set of two loops, loosely shaped in a figure 8, runs 2.5-miles round trip to Red Granite Falls in the park's southern corner. It's also listed as the Red Trail on the park's winter maps.

To reach the state park, from Mellen, take Wis. Hwy. 169 north. Enter the park by turning left onto Copper Falls Road, and park in the Loon Lake Beach lot. Head south to the beach and pick up the trailhead heading west.

A popular destination at the park, Loon Lake offers a sand beach, swimming area, and canoe launch. Fishermen often can be spotted vying for largemouth bass, northern pike and panfish there.

From the beach, the trail curves away from Loon Lake. It crosses a road and then intersects with a connecting trail going right/north. Shortly beyond that intersection, the trail enters its first loop; at that point, go right/west.

Because of the park's diversity in trees, a great time to hike the trail is autumn. You'll find the brilliant yellows of ironwood, paper birch and aspen, the blazing orange of sugar maple, and the scarlet of red oak mixed with the evergreen of hemlock and white pine. White cedars line the riverway.

Half-way through the loop, the trail reaches a connector linking the two loops. Head right/southwest onto the connector.

With all of the tree cover, you're likely to spot and certainly see the signs of a variety of animals, including white-tailed deer, porcupines, fishers, raccoons, black bears, wood frogs, and red squirrels. Up to 200 bird species migrate through the park during spring and fall; northern ravens, great pileated woodpecker, chickadees, ruffed grouse, eagles, and loons are common. Each June and July, banded purple and tiger swallowtail butterflies descend upon the woodlands.

When the connector reaches the second loop, go right/west. You're a little more than half-way on the loop to the Bad River once you pass beneath the power line. As the trail curves south, you'll find yourself on the river's shores.

The Bad River tumbles over red granite boulders, in what is more of a rapids than a falls, alongside the trail. Though slippery, older children with adults can safely walk onto some of the rocks in the rapids.

Red Granite Falls owes its existence to lava flows from a billion years ago. For the past 200 million years, the Bad River has ran, except during glaciation, over the hardened lava or the sediment above it.

In addition to the great geological scenery, the Bad River is an excellent place to fish for rainbow, brown and brook trout.

When the trail curves east away from the river, you're on the route way back. To ensure you hike the parts of the loops not done on the way in, always go right at the trail intersections.

During winter, the trail is rolled with a snow-mobile for snowshoeing and cold weather hiking. Cross country skiing also is allowed.

One final note, if you have a four-legged friend in your family: Dogs are welcomed on the trail, even during winter.

Other Ashland County Trails

■ **Doughboys' Nature Trail** – Hikers can tour Wisconsin's geological history in some of the most breathtaking scenery this side of the Mississippi on Doughboys' Nature Trail at Copper Falls State Park. The 1.7-mile loop follows the Bad River and Tyler Forks past Copper and Brownstone waterfalls and a series of cascades.

■ **North Country National Scenic Trail, Copper Falls State Park segment** – Waterfalls, Northwoods lakes, and sandstone ledges await day hikers on a segment of the North Country National Scenic Trail in Copper Falls State Park. An excellent 5-miles round trip segment of the trail that includes most of the park's highlights runs from Loon Lake to the Sandstone Ledges. The trail can be picked up at the Loon Lake parking lot.

■ **West Torch Trail** – Hikers can escape modern

life into a thick, serene woods on the West Torch Trail south of Clam Lake in the Chequamegon National Forest. Wild Torch is a stacked loop trail system with loop lengths of 0.8, 1.7, 3.7, and five miles. The longer two loops offer some hilly terrain, but combining the 0.8 and 1.7 loops makes for an easy 2.2-mile hike (The loops share a stretch of trail.).

■ Also see *Ashland* above.

Sawyer County

A recreation mecca, Sawyer County sits in the heart of the Wisconsin Northwoods. Every winter, tens of thousands of cross-country skiers descend upon its county seat, Hayward, for the annual Birkebeiner race, North America's most popular cross country ski marathon. During summer, off-road mountain bike riders flock to Sawyer County for the annual Chequamegon Fat Tire Festival, the nation's largest mass start mountain bike race. Depending upon the season, on any given day campers, fishing boats, and snowmobiles criss-cross the landscape. All of these cross country, mountain bike and snowmobile trails, campgrounds, and clear blue lakes also make for great day hiking opportunities.

Totagatic River State Wildlife Area Jeep Trail
Totagatic River State Wildlife Area

Day hikers can ramble alongside one of Wisconsin's few remaining wilderness streams on a jeep trail in the Totagatic River State Wildlife Area.

Though not a designated trail, the old logging road runs about a mile (2-miles round trip) through a forested area along the Totagatic Flowage's northwest side. The flowage marks a wide swath of the meandering Totagatic River, which in 2009 became Wisconsin's fifth stream to receive Wild River status.

To reach the trailhead, from Hayward take Wis. Hwy. 77 north/west. Turn left/north onto Wis. Hwy. 27. Park off the road on the west side of Hwy. 27 across from Dam Road. The jeep trail heads northwest from the parking area.

Most of the trail is under the cover of northern hardwoods, which makes for a scenic walk during autumn.

The Totagatic runs 70 miles through five counties. Its headwaters are in southern Bayfield County. Popular among canoeists, the cold and clear river flows into Totagatic Lake then to Nelson Lake and into the flowage. Hwy. 27 and the dam split Nelson Lake from the flowage.

Expect to spot a number of waterfowl along the hike. The bird-friendly flowage was constructed in the 1950s, and the 272-acre Totagatic River Wildlife Area has long been designated a state waterfowl restoration area. A mix of habitats – from hardwood forests and open water to swamps and upland grasslands – make up the wildlife area.

If you ask locals about the river or read printed materials on it, you're likely to run into some

confusing appellations. Spellings and pronunciations of the river are about as murky as its name
suggests – "Totagatic" is derived from the Ojibwa
word "Totogan," which translates as "boggy river." Maps, plat books, tour guides variously spell
the river's name as "Totagatic" and "Totogatic."
Local pronunciations range from "Tuh-TO-ga-tec"
and "To-TA-ga-tec" to "To-to-GAT-ic" and "To-BA-
tec."

From the flowage, the river heads roughly west.
Northwest of Minong, it turns south and eventually
flows into the Namekagon River.

Back in the wildlife area, the trail peters out at the
edge of the flowage, a grasslands that the river
runs through the center of. As an old logging road,
expect parts of the trail to be overgrown, so don
jeans and insect repellent for the hike.

Other Sawyer County Trails

■ **Birkie Ridge Trail** – A new route in the massive Birkebeiner Trail system, the 2.9-mile round
trip Birkie Ridge opened in August 2013, running
entirely through a northern hardwood forest that's
particularly colorful in autumn. The trailhead is on
the east side of U.S. Hwy. 63 north of the Northern
Lights Road junction.

■ **Black Lake Trail** – Hikers can learn about the
history of Northwoods logging while enjoying excellent water views on the Black Lake Trail in Sawyer and Ashland counties. Most of the Chequa-

megon National Forest's Black Lake is in Ashland County – though to get there you'll probably spend most of your time driving through Sawyer County. It's on Forest Road 174 (Barker Lake Road outside of the national forest), north of County Road B.

■ **Blue and Orange trails** – Among the Northwoods' newest hiking trails can be found at the Town of Hayward Recreational Forest west of Hayward. The 160-acre facility opened in spring 2011 and is quickly becoming a popular cross country skiing, snowshoeing and day hiking desti-nation. Combining the rec forest's Blue and Orange trails into a 1.6-mile walk takes you through a woods past a wetland and then a scenic lake where wildlife is abundant. Dogs are welcomed.

■ **Namekagon-Laccourt Oreilles Portage Trail** – The easy, 0.8-mile loop memorializes a famous 18th century route where fur traders and explorers carried their canoes between rivers. The trailhead in the St. Croix National Scenic Riverway is on Rolf Road west of Rainbow Road.

■ **Kissick Swamp Wildlife Area North Trail** – Park at the Kissick Swamp Wildlife Area lot on the south side of West Chippnazie Lake Road, west of the intersection with Company Lake Road. A trail winds for about a half-mile one-way (1-mile round trip) through woodlands on the wildlife area's north side.

■ **Pacwawong Lake Trail** – Less a walking path than a jeep trail for boat ramp access to Pacwawong Lake in the scenic riverway, this 0.4-mile round trip is remote enough that there won't be much if any traffic. From Cable Sunset/Totalatic Road, head south on Mossback Road, taking the first left/east; park in the gravel lot at the boat ramp and walk back to the road.

■ **Timber Lawn Trail** – The 1.2-mile round trip southwest of Hayward runs through woods to an overlook of the Namekagon's north shore in the scenic riverway. From Old 24/Nursery Road (which parallels U.S. Hwy. 63), take Timber Lawn Road south until it becomes a jeep trail, where you can park. You can extend the trail by making a loop from the overlook via the jeep trail that heads north back to your vehicle.

■ Also see this series' sister book, *Day Hiking Trails of Sawyer County, Wisconsin.*

Douglas County

L ocated west of Bayfield County in Wisconsin's northwest corner, Douglas County offers a number of outdoors attractions perfect for day hikers. Two state parks with waterfalls, long stretches of the St. Croix National Scenic Riverway, and the Brule River State Forest that spills into Lake Superior, all offer a number of scenic hiking trails. A number of excellent trails, including those that meander along the Lake Superior, can be found in Superior and just across the state line in Duluth, Minn.

Stoney Hill Nature Trail
Brule River State Forest

A short loop trail offers fantastic views of northern Wisconsin's Brule River Valley.

The Stoney Hill Nature Trail runs 1.7-miles in the Brule River State Forest. If staying overnight at the Bois Brule Campground, the sunrise seen from atop Stoney Hill definitely is worth getting up early for.

To reach the trailhead, from Iron River take U.S. Hwy. 2 west about six miles past Brule. Turn left/

south onto Ranger Road, following it for a little more than a mile to the ranger station on the banks of the Bois Brule River. Parking is available at the station. From there, take the connector heading south to the nature trail.

As the river sits at about 950 feet elevation near the station, you'll have some climbing to do to reach the top of Stoney Hill. Parts of the trail will be steep.

One of the country's best coldwater trout streams, the Bois Brule also is a favorite of paddlers. Salmon can be found in the river, which meanders from wetlands near Upper St. Croix Lake then to Lake Superior for 44 miles and drops 328 feet along the way.

The Bois Brule for many years was popular with outdoors-minded U.S. presidents. Privately-owned Cedar Island Lodge hosted five U.S. presidents – Ulysses Grant, Grover Cleveland, Calvin Coolidge, Herbert Hoover, and Dwight Eisenhower – with Coolidge spending the summer of 1928 there. Because of this, the Bois Brule has been nicknamed the "river of presidents."

Interpretive signs along the nature trail describe the various trees found in the state forest. A variety of hardwoods, including oak, can be seen, and part of the trail-heads through a pine plantation.

The top of Stoney Hill is at 1181 feet elevation and today hosts a radio tower and overlook. From the summit are good views of the Bois Brule River with its Little Joe Rapids to the west and Doodlebug Rapids to the north, Hoodoo Lake to the south, and the Little Bois Brule River to the east.

Though pets are allowed in the state forest, they cannot be taken on this trail.

Brule Bog Boardwalk Trail
Brule River State Forest

Visitors to the Solon Springs area can day hike what feels like the forest primeval on the Brule Bog Boardwalk Trail.

Located in southern Douglas County's Brule River State Forest, the 2.3-mile boardwalk cuts through a wooded bog. Part of the North Country National Scenic Trail, it is entirely handicapped accessible.

To reach the trail, from downtown Solon Springs take County Road A north for about three miles, rounding the northern side of Upper St. Croix Lake. Watch for signs saying the North Country Trail is "1000 Feet Ahead," then turn into the boat landing where you can park.

Across the road from the parking lot, the trail heading right/northeast is the Brule-St. Croix Portage Trail (see below). The boardwalk trail heads left or directly north.

An elevated boardwalk takes hikers through a coifer swamp at the bottom of a narrow valley. The valley marks a continental divide – all rivers to the south ultimately feed the Mississippi River while those to the north flow into Lake Superior, which is part of the St. Lawrence watershed.

In short order, the boardwalk crosses St. Croix Creek. You've now entered the heart of Brule Bog. Ferns and mosses, as well as several varieties of orchids, cover the ground while white cedar, balsam fir, and spruce crowd out the sunlight.

Several rare plants and animals can be found in the bog. Among the insects you'll quickly notice is the zebra clubtail dragonfly. Songbirds include the black-backed woodpecker, golden-crowned kinglet, Lincoln's sparrow, olive-sided flycatcher, and saw-whet owl. Plants include the sheathed and the sparse-flowered sedge and the endangered Lapland buttercup.

The sense of having traveled back in time to the ancient Carboniferous Period is temporarily interrupted as the trail crosses County Road P, which runs smack down the bog's middle.

After the county road, the boardwalk trail veers northwest. You'll come to the edge of the bog against a hillside, where the trail begins to meander. The uplands above the bog consist of sandy pine barrens.

Some 9,000 years ago as the last ice age ended, a river flowing from the much higher glacial Lake Superior carved out the valley where the Brule River, this bog, and Upper St. Croix Lake now exist. Released from the retreating glacier's weight, the land rose, causing water to flow in opposite directions and hence the divide.

The boardwalk ends at a spur off of Croshaw Road. This is the turnaround point.

A final note: You'll definitely want to apply insect repellent before hitting this trail.

Other Douglas County Trails

■ **Amnicon Falls Island Trails** – Hikers can view the results of an earthquake from 500 million years ago while walking the island trails at Amnicon Falls State Park. Among the sites are three waterfalls and a covered bridge.

■ **Bayfield Road Trail** – The 2.25-mile loop trail in the Brule River State Forest passes through red oak stands that recently came under attack by the two-lined chestnut borer, offering insights into the woodlands and a tree species man is trying to rescue. A connecting trail leads to the Copper Range Campground.

■ **Big Manitou Falls Overlook Trails** – Though a good drive from Bayfield County, the trail is worth it, as it boasts 165-foot Big Manitou Falls, the fourth highest waterfall east of the Rockies and Wisconsin's tallest. The waterfalls is in Pattison State Park south of Superior.

■ **Brule-St. Croix Portage Trail** – People have used this trail for hundreds of years, most notably beginning in 1680 when French explorer Daniel Greysolon Sieur duLhut first noted the route linking the Brule and St. Croix rivers. The path north of

Solon Springs is an easy 4.4-mile out-and-back trail with minimal elevation gain.

■ **North Country National Scenic Trail, Brule River State Forest segment** – The scenic trail runs roughly north-south through the lower half of the Brule River State Forest. A peaceful segment to walk is from Wis. Hwy. 27 (north of Radio Station Road) south to County Road S for a six-mile round trip.

■ **North Country National Scenic Trail, Douglas County Forest segment** – South of Solon Springs, the seven-state North Country Trail crosses the Douglas County Forest for roughly three miles. It passes several idyllic ponds along the way.

■ **North Country National Scenic Trail, segment through Solon Springs** – Before reaching the county forest, the trail cuts through the village. A pleasant two-mile route runs south of town to the county forest from South Holly Lucius Road/U.S. Hwy. 53 to Bird Sanctuary Road at the forest's edge.

■ **Thimbleberry Nature Trail** – Thick with a variety of trees and wildlife, this 0.8-mile trail at Amnicon Falls State Park includes a side trip to a pond that at one time was a brownstone quarry.

■ **Tri-County Corridor Trail** – Connecting Superior to Ashland, the trail heads through Poplar. To get away from the highway noise, try the roughly 2.25-mile one-way segment between Midway

Road and County Road F.

■ **Wild Rivers State Trail segment** – The rail line turned hiking path also runs through Solon Springs on its way between Gordon and Superior. To avoid highway noise, take the roughly four-mile route heading north from the municipal airport to County Road L.

Best Trails

Which Bayfield County trails are the best for watching birds? Getting around on a wheelchair? Walking the family dog? Here are some lists of the best trails for those and many other specific interests.

Autumn leaves
- Drummond Woods Interpretative Trail
- Lake Owen Loop
- Namekagon Dam Landing Trail

Beaches/waterways
- Bay View Trail (Madeline Island)
- Lakeshore Trail
- Sioux River Flats Beach Trail

Birdwatching
- Houghton Falls Trail
- Jerry Jolly Hiking Trail
- Teuton Trail Loop C

Dog-friendly
- Blue and Orange trails (Sawyer County)
- Red Granite Falls Trail (Ashland County)

Campgrounds
- Birch Grove Campground Trail
- Lake Owen Loop
- Two Lakes Campground Trail

Geology
- Brownstone Trail
- Houghton Falls Trail
- Lakeshore Mainland Trail
- Morgan Falls St. Peter's Dome Trail (Ashland County)

Handicap accessible
- Brule Bog Boardwalk Trail (Douglas County)
- Interpretive Boardwalk Trail

History/Archeology
- Black Lake Trail (Ashland/Sawyer County)
- Forest Road 1919B/BA Trail
- Namekagon-Laccourt Oreilles Portage Trail (Sawyer County)

Lakes (inland)
- Erick Lake segment (North Country National Scenic Trail)
- Lake Owen Loop
- Namekagon Dam Landing Trail

Lake Superior views
- Bay View Trail (Madeline Island)

- Brownstone Trail
- Cornucopia Walking Trail
- Houghton Falls Trail
- Lakeshore Trail

Must-do's
- Drummond Woods Interpretative Trail
- Forest Lodge Nature Trail
- Houghton Falls Trail
- Lakeshore Mainland Trail
- North Country National Scenic Trail (Lake Owen Loop)

Picnicing
- Bay View Trail (Madeline Island)
- Lake Owen Loop
- Long Lake Picnic Area Trail

Plant communities
- Drummond Woods Interpretative Trail
- Forest Lodge Nature Trail
- Interpretive Boardwalk Trail

Swimming
- Lake Owen Loop
- Red Granite Falls Trail (Ashland County)

Vistas
- Bay View Trail (Madeline Island)
- Houghton Falls Trail

■ Morgan Falls St. Peter's Dome Trail (Ashland County)

Waterfalls
■ Amnicon Falls Island Trails (Douglas County)
■ Big Manitou Falls Overlook Trails (Douglas County)
■ Doughboys' Nature Trail (Ashland County)
■ Houghton Falls Trail
■ Morgan Falls St. Peter's Dome Trail (Ashland County)

Wildlife
■ Interpretive Boardwalk Trail
■ Lake Owen Loop (North Country National Scenic Trail)
■ Namekagon Trail East Loop

Bonus Section:
Day Hiking Primer

Y ou'll get more out of a day hike if you research it and plan ahead. It's not enough to
just pull over to the side of the road and hit a
trail that you've never been on and have no idea
where it goes. In fact, doing so invites disaster.

Instead, you should preselect a trail (This book's
trail descriptions can help you do that). You'll also
want to ensure that you have the proper clothing,
equipment, navigational tools, first-aid kit, food
and water. Knowing the rules of the trail and poten-
tial dangers along the way also are helpful. In this
special section, we'll look at each of these topics to
ensure you're fully prepared.

Selecting a trail

For your first few hikes, stick to short, well-
known trails where you're likely to encounter others. Once you get a feel for hiking, your abilities,
and your interests, expand to longer and more remote trails.

Always check to see what the weather will be
like on the trail you plan to hike. While an adult

might be able to withstand wind and a sprinkle here or there, if you bring children, for them it can be pure misery. Dry, pleasantly warm days with limited wind always are best when hiking with children.

Don't choose a trail that is any longer than the least fit person in your group can hike. Adults in good shape can go 8-12 miles a day; for kids, it's much less. There's no magical number.

When planning the hike, try to find a trail with a mid-point payoff – that is something you and definitely any children will find exciting about halfway through the hike. This will help keep up everyone's energy and enthusiasm up during the journey.

If you have children in your hiking party, consider a couple of additional points when selecting a trail.

Until children enter their late teens, they need to stick to trails rather than going off-trail hiking, which is known as bushwhacking. Children too easily can get lost when off trail. They also can easily get scratched and cut up or stumble across poisonous plants and dangerous animals.

Generally, kids will prefer a circular route to one that requires hiking back the way you came. A return on an out-and-back trail often feels anti-climatic, but you can beat that by mentioning features that all of you might want to take a closer look at.

Once you select a trail, it's time to plan for your

day hike. Doing so will save you a lot of grief – and potentially prevent an emergency – later on. You are, after all, entering the wilds, a place where help may not be readily available.

When planning your hike, follow these steps:

- Print a road map showing how to reach the parking lot near the trailhead. Outline the route with a transparent yellow highlighter and write out the directions.
- Print a satellite photo of the parking area and the trailhead. Mark the trailhead on the photo.
- Print a topo map of the trail. Outline the trail with the yellow highlighter. Note interesting features you want to see along the trail and the destination.
- If carrying GPS, program this information into your device.
- Make a timeline for your trip, listing: when you will leave home; when you will arrive at the trailhead; your turnback time; when you will return for home in your vehicle; and when you will arrive at your home.
- Estimate how much water and food you will need to bring based on the amount of time you plan to spend on the trail and in your vehicle. You'll need at least 2 pints of water per person for every hour on the trail.
- Fill out two copies of a hiker's safety form. Leave one in your vehicle.

■ Share all of this information with a responsible person remaining in civilization, leaving a hiker's safety form with them. If they do not hear from you within an hour of when you plan to leave the trail in your vehicle, they should contact authorities to report you as possibly lost.

Clothing
Footwear

If your feet hurt, the hike is over, so getting the right footwear is worth the time. Making sure the footwear fits before hitting the trail also is worth it. With children, if you've gone a few weeks without hiking, that's plenty of time for feet to grow, and they may have just outgrown their hiking boots. Check out everyone's footwear a few days before heading out on the hike. If it doesn't fit, replace it.

For flat, smooth, dry trails, sneakers and cross-trainers are fine; but if you really want to head onto less traveled roads or tackle areas that aren't typically dry, you'll need hiking boots. Once you start doing any rocky or steep trails – and remember that a trail you consider moderately steep needs to be only half that angle for a child to consider it extremely steep – you'll want hiking boots, which offer rugged tread perfect for handling rough trails.

Socks

Socks serve two purposes: to wick sweat away

from skin and to provide cushioning. Cotton socks aren't very good for hiking, except in extremely dry environments, because they retain moisture that can result in blisters. Wool socks or liner socks work best. You'll want to look for three-season socks, also known as trekking socks. While a little thicker than summer socks, their extra cushioning generally prevents blisters. Also, make sure kids don't put on holey socks; that's just inviting blisters.

Layering

On all but the hot, dry days, when hiking you should wear multiple layers of clothing that provide various levels of protection against sweat, heat loss, wind and potentially rain. Layering works because the type of clothing you select for each stratum serves a different function, such as wicking moisture or shielding against wind. In addition, trapped air between each layer of clothing is warmed by your body heat. Layers also can be added or taken off as needed.

Generally, you need three layers. Closest to your skin is the wicking layer, which pulls perspiration away from the body and into the next layer, where it evaporates. Exertion from walking means you will sweat and generate heat, even if the weather is cold. The second layer is an insulation layer, which helps keep you warm. The last layer is a water-resistant shell that protects you from rain, wind, snow and sleet.

As the seasons and weather change, so does the type of clothing you select for each layer. The first layer ought to be a loose-fitting T-shirt in summer, but in winter and on other cold days you might opt for a long-sleeved moisture-wicking synthetic material, like polypropylene. During winter, the next layer probably also should cover the neck, which often is exposed to the elements. A turtleneck works fine, but preferably not one made of cotton. The third layer in winter, depending on the temperature, could be a wool sweater, a half-zippered long sleeved fleece jacket, or a fleece vest.

You might even add a fourth layer of a hooded parka with pockets, made of material that can block wind and resist water. Gloves or mittens as well as a hat also are necessary on cold days.

Headgear

Half of all body heat is lost through the head, hence the hiker's adage, "If your hands are cold, wear a hat." In cool, wet weather, wearing a hat is at least good for avoiding hypothermia, a potentially deadly condition in which heat loss occurs faster than the body can generate it. Children are more susceptible to hypothermia than adults.

Especially during summer, a hat with a wide brim is useful in keeping the sun out of your eyes. It's also nice should rain start to fall.

For young children, get a hat with a chin strap.

They like to play with their hats, which will fly off in a wind gust if not "fastened" some way to the child.

Sunglasses

Sunglasses are an absolute must when walking through open areas exposed to the sun and in winter when you can suffer from snow blindness. Look for 100% UV-protective shades, which provide the best screen.

Equipment

A couple of principles should guide your purchases. First, the longer and more complex the hike, the more equipment you'll need. Secondly, your general goal is to go light. Since you're on a day hike, the amount of gear you'll need is a fraction of what backpackers shown in magazines and catalogues usually carry. Indeed, the inclination of most day hikers is to not carry enough equipment. For the lightness issue, most gear today is made with titanium and siliconized nylon, ensuring it is sturdy yet light. While the list of what you need may look long, it won't weigh much.

Backpacks

Sometimes called daypacks (for day hikes or for kids), backpacks are essential to carry all of the essentials you need – snacks, first-aid kit, extra clothing.

For day hike purposes, you'll want to get yourself an internal frame, in which the frame giving the backpack its shape is inside the pack's fabric so it's not exposed to nature. Such frames usually are lightweight and comfortable. External frames have the frame outside the pack, so they are exposed to the elements. They are excellent for long hikes into the backcountry when you must carry heavy loads.

As kids get older, and especially after they've been hiking for a couple of years, they'll soon want a "real" backpack. Unfortunately, most backpacks for kids are overbuilt and too heavy. Even light ones that safely can hold up to 50 pounds are inane for most children.

When buying a daypack for your child, look for sternum straps, which help keep the strap on the shoulders. This is vital for prepubescent children as they do not have the broad shoulders that come with adolescence, meaning packs likely will slip off and onto their arms, making them uncomfortable and difficult to carry. Don't buy a backpack that a child will "grow into." Backpacks that don't fit well simply will lead to sore shoulder and back muscles and could result in poor posture.

Also, consider purchasing a daypack with a hydration system for kids. This will help ensure they drink a lot of water. More on this later when we get to canteens.

Before hitting the trail, always check your children's backpacks to make sure that they have not overloaded them. Kids think they need more than they really do. They also tend to overestimate their own ability to carry stuff. Sibling rivalries often lead to children to packing more than they should in their rucksacks, too. Don't let them overpack "to teach them a lesson," though, as it can damage bones and turn the hike into a bad experience.

A good rule of thumb is no more than 25 percent capacity. Most upper elementary school kids can carry only about 10 pounds for any short distance. Subtract the weight of the backpack, and that means only 4-5 pounds in the backpack. Overweight children will need to carry a little less than this or they'll quickly be out of breath.

Child carriers

If your child is an infant or toddler, you'll have to carry him. Until infants can hold their heads up, which usually doesn't happen until about four to six months of age, a front pack (like a Snugli or Baby Bjorn) is best. It keeps the infant close for warmth and balances out your backpack. At the same time, though, you must watch for baby overheating in a front pack, so you'll need to remove the infant from your body at rest stops.

Once children reach about 20 pounds, they typically can hold their heads up and sit on their own. At that point, you'll want a baby carrier (sometimes called a child carrier or baby backpack), which can transfer the infant's weight to your hips when you walk. You'll not only be comfortable, but your child will love it, too.

Look for a baby carrier that is sturdy yet lightweight. Your child is going to get heavier as time passes, so about the only way you can counteract this is to reduce the weight of the items you use to carry things. The carrier also should have adjustment points, as you don't want your child to outgrow the carrier too soon. A padded waist belt and padded shoulder straps are necessary for your comfort. The carrier should provide some kind of head and neck support if you're hauling an infant. It also should offer back support for children of all ages, and leg holes should be wide enough so there's no chafing. You want to be able to load your infant without help, so it should be stable enough to stand so when you take it off the child can sit in it for a moment while you get turned around. Stay away from baby carriers with only shoulder straps as you need the waist belt to help shift the child's weight to your hips for more comfortable walking.

Fanny packs

Also known as a belt bag, a fanny pack is virtually a must for anyone with a baby carrier as you can't otherwise carry a backpack. If your significant other is with you, he or she can carry the backpack, of course. Still, the fanny pack also is a good alternative to a backpack in hot weather, as it will reduce back sweat.

If you have only one or two kids on a hike, or if they also are old enough to carry daypacks, your fanny pack need not be large. A mid-size pouch can carry at least 200 cubic inches of supplies, which is more than enough to accommodate all the materials you need. A good fanny pack also has a place to hook canteens to it.

Canteens

Canteens or plastic bottles filled with water are vital for any hike, no matter how short the trail. You'll need to have enough of them to carry about two pints of water per person for every hour of hiking.

Trekking poles

Also known as walking poles or walking sticks, trekking poles are necessary for maintaining stability on uneven or wet surfaces and to help reduce fatigue. The latter makes them useful on even surfaces. By transferring weight to the arms, a trekking pole can reduce stress on knees and lower back, allowing you to maintain a better posture and to go farther.

If you're carrying a baby or toddler on your back, you'll primarily want a trekking pole to help you maintain your balance, even if on a flat surface, and to help absorb some of the impact of your step.

Graphite tips provide the best traction. A basket

just above the tip is a good idea so the stick doesn't sink into mud or sand. Angled cork handles are ergonomic and help absorb sweat from your hands so they don't blister. A strap on the handle to wrap around your hand is useful so the stick doesn't slip out. Telescopic poles are a good idea as you can adjust them as needed based on the terrain you're hiking and as kids grow to accommodate their height.

The pole also needs to be sturdy enough to handle rugged terrain, as you don't want a pole that bends when you press it to the ground. Spring-loaded shock absorbers help when heading down a steep incline but aren't necessary. Indeed, for a short walk across flat terrain, the right length stick is about all you need.

Carabiners

Carabiners are metal loops, vaguely shaped like a D, with a sprung or screwed gate. You'll find that hooking a couple of them to your backpack or fanny pack useful in many ways. For example, if you need to dig through a fanny pack, you can hook the strap of your trekking pole to it. Your hat, camera straps, first-aid kit, and a number of other objects also can connect to them. Hook carabiners to your fanny pack or backpack upon purchasing them, so you don't forget them when packing. Small carabiners with sprung gates are inexpensive, but they do have a limited life span of a couple of dozen hikes.

Navigational tools

Paper maps

Paper maps may sound passé in this age of GPS, but you'll find the variety and breadth of view they offer to be useful. During the planning process, a paper map (even if viewing it online), will be far superior to a GPS device. On the hike, you'll also want a backup to GPS. Or like many casual hikers, you may not own GPS at all, which makes paper maps indispensable.

Standard road maps (which includes printed guides and handmade trail maps) show highways and locations of cities and parks. Maps included in guidebooks, printed guides handed out at parks, and those that are hand-drawn tend to be designed like road maps, and often carry the same positives and negatives.

Topographical maps give contour lines and other important details for crossing a landscape. You'll find them invaluable on a hike into the wilds. The contour lines' shape and their spacing on a topo map show the form and steepness of a hill or bluff, unlike the standard road map and most brochures and hand-drawn trail maps. You'll also know if you're in a woods, which is marked in green, or in a clearing, which is marked in white. If you get lost, figuring out where you are and how to get to where you need to be will be much easier with such information.

Satellite photos offer a view from above that is rendered exactly as it would look from an airplane. Thanks to Google and other online services, you can get fairly detailed pictures of the landscape. Such pictures are an excellent resource when researching a hiking trail. Unfortunately, those pictures don't label what a feature is or what it's called, as would a topo map. Unless there's a stream, determining if a feature is a valley bottom or a ridgeline also can be difficult. Like topo maps, satellite photos (most of which were taken by old Russian spy satellites), can be out of date a few years.

GPS

By using satellites, the global positioning system can find your spot on the Earth to within 10 feet. With a GPS device, you can preprogram the trailhead location and mark key turns and landmarks as well as the hike's end point. This mobile map is a powerful technological tool that almost certainly ensures you won't get lost – so long as you've correctly programmed the information. GPS also can calculate travel time and act as a compass, a barometer and altimeter, making such devices virtually obsolete on a hike.

In remote areas, however, reception is spotty at best for GPS, rendering your mobile map worthless. A GPS device also runs on batteries, and there's always a chance they will go dead. Or you may drop your device, breaking it in the process. Their screens are small, and sometimes you need a large paper map to get a good sense of the natural landmarks around you.

Compass

Like a paper map, a compass is indispensable even if you use GPS. Should your GPS no longer function, the compass then can be used to tell you which direction you're heading. A protractor compass is best for hiking. Beneath the compass needle is a transparent base with lines to help your orient yourself. The compass often serves as a magnifying glass to help you make out map details. Most protractor compasses also come with a lanyard for easy carrying.

Food and water

Water

As water is the heaviest item you'll probably carry, there is a temptation to not take as much as one should. Don't skimp on the amount of water you bring, though; after all, it's the one supply your body most needs. It's always better to end up with extra water than returning to your vehicle dehydrated.

How much water should you take? Adults need at least a quart for every two hours hiking. Children need to drink about a quart every two hours of walking and more if the weather is hot or dry. To keep kids hydrated, have them drink at every rest stop.

Don't presume there will be water on the hiking trail. Most trails outside of urban areas lack such amenities. In addition, don't drink water from local streams, lakes, rivers or ponds. There's no way to tell if local water is safe or not. As soon as you have drunk half of your water supply, you should turn around for the vehicle.

Food

Among the many wonderful things about hiking is that snacking between meals isn't frowned upon. Unless going on an all-day hike in which you'll picnic along the way, you want to keep everyone in your hiking party fed, especially as hunger can lead to lethargic and discontented children. It'll also keep young kids from snacking on the local flora or dirt. Before hitting the trail, you'll want to repackage as much of the food as possible as products sold at grocery stores tend to come in bulky packages that take up space and add a little weight to your backpack. Place the food in resealable plastic bags.

Bring a variety of small snacks for rest stops. You don't want kids filling up on snacks, but you do need them to maintain their energy levels if they're walking or to ensure they don't turn fussy if riding in a child carrier. Go for complex carbohydrates and proteins for maintaining energy. Good options include dried fruits, jerky, nuts, peanut butter, pre-pared energy bars, candy bars with a high protein content (nuts, peanut butter), crackers, raisins and trail mix (called "gorp"). A number of trail mix rec-ipes are available online (*hikeswithtykes.blogspot. com*); you and your children may want to try them out at home to see which ones you collectively like most.

Salty treats rehydrate better than sweet treats do. Chocolate and other sweets are fine if they're not all that's exclusively served, but remember they also tend to lead to thirst and to make sticky messes. Whichever snacks you choose, don't ex-periment with food on the trail. Bring what you know kids will like.

Give the first snack within a half-hour of leaving the trailhead or you risk children becoming tired and whiny from low energy levels. If kids start ask-ing for them every few steps even after having something to eat at the last rest stop, consider timing snacks to reaching a seeable landmark, such as, "We'll get out the trail mix when we reach that bend up ahead."

Milk for infants

If you have an infant or unweaned toddler with you, milk is as necessary as water. Children who only drink breastfed milk but don't have their mother on the hike require that you have breast-pumped milk in an insulated beverage container (such as a Thermos) that can keep it cool to avoid spoiling. Know how much the child drinks and at what frequency so you can bring enough. You'll also need to carry the child's bottle and feeding nipples. Bring enough extra water in your canteen so you can wash out the bottle after each feeding. A handkerchief can be used to dry bottles between feedings.

Don't forget the baby's pacifier. Make sure it has a string and hook on it so it connects to the baby's outfit and isn't lost.

What not to bring

Avoid soda and other caffeinated beverages, alcohol, and energy pills. The caffeine will dehydrate children as well as you. Alcohol has no place on the trail; you need your full faculties when making decisions and driving home. Energy pills essentially are a stimulant and like alcohol can lead to bad calls. If you're tired, get some sleep and hit the trail another day.

First-aid kit

After water, this is the most essential item you can carry.

A first-aid kit should include:

■ Adhesive bandages of various types and sizes, especially butterfly bandages (for younger kids, make sure they're colorful kid bandages)

■ Aloe vera

■ Anesthetic (such as Benzocaine)
■ Antacid (tablets)
■ Antibacterial (aka antibiotic) ointment (such as Neosporin or Bacitracin)
■ Anti-diarrheal tablets (for adults only, as giving this to a child is controversial)
■ Anti-itch cream or calamine lotion
■Antiseptics (such as hydrogen peroxide, iodine or Betadine, Mercuroclear, rubbing alcohol)
■ Baking soda
■ Breakable (or instant) ice packs
■ Cotton swabs
■ Disposable syringe (w/o needle)
■ Epipen (if children or adults have allergies)
■ Fingernail clippers (your multi-purpose tool might have this, and if so you can dispense with it)
■ Gauze bandage
■ Gauze compress pads (2x2 individually wrapped pad)
■ Hand sanitizer (use this in place of soap)
■ Liquid antihistamine (not Benadryl tablets, however, as children should take liquid not pills; be aware that liquid antihistamines may cause drowsiness)
■ Medical tape
■ Moisturizer containing an anti-inflammatory
■ Mole skin
■ Pain reliever (a.k.a. aspirin; for children's pain relief, use liquid acetaminophen such Tylenol or liquid ibuprofen; never give aspirin to a child

under 12)
- Poison ivy cream (for treatment)
- Poison ivy soap
- Powdered sports drinks mix or electrolyte additives
- Sling
- Snakebite kit
- Thermometer
- Tweezers (your multi-purpose tool may have this allowing you to dispense with it)
- Water purification tablets

If infants are with you, be sure to also carry teething ointment (such as Orajel) and diaper rash treatment.

Many of the items should be taken out of their store packaging to make placement in your fanny pack or backpack easier. In addition, small amounts of some items – such as baking soda and cotton swabs – can be placed inside re-sealable plastic bags, since you won't need the whole amount purchased.

Make sure the first-aid items are in a waterproof container. A re-sealable plastic zipper bag is perfectly fine. As Bayfield County sports a humid climate, be sure to replace the adhesive bandages every couple of months, as they can deteriorate in the moistness. Also, check your first-aid kit every few trips and after any hike in which you've just used it, so that you can replace used components and to make sure medicines haven't expired.

If you have older elementary-age kids and teen-agers who've been trained in first aid, giving them a kit to carry as well as yourself is a good idea. Should they find themselves lost or if you cannot get to them for a few moments, the kids might need to provide very basic first aid to one another.

Hiking with children: Attitude adjustment

To enjoy hiking with kids, you'll first have to adopt your child's perspective. Simply put, we must learn to hike on our kids' schedules – even though they may not know that's what we're doing.

Compared to adults, kids can't walk as far, they can't walk as fast, and they will grow bored more quickly. Every step we take requires three for them. In addition, early walkers, up to 2 years of age, prefer to wander than to "hike." Preschool kids will start to walk the trail, but at a rate of only about a mile per hour. With stops, that can turn a three-mile hike into a four-hour journey. Kids also won't be able to hike as steep of trails as you or handle as inclement of weather as you might.

This all may sound limiting, especially to long-time backpackers used to racking up miles or bag-ging peaks on their hikes, but it's really not. While you may have to put off some backcountry and mountain climbing trips for a while, it also opens up to you a number of great short trails and nature hikes with spectacular sights that you may have otherwise skipped because they weren't challeng–

ing enough.

So sure, you'll have to make some compromises, but the payout is high. You're not personally on the hike to get a workout but to spend quality time with your children.

Family dog

Dogs are part of the family, and if you have children, they'll want to share the hiking experience with their pets. In turn, dogs will have a blast on the trail, some larger dogs can be used as Sherpas, and others will defend against threatening animals.

But there is a downside to dogs. Many will chase animals and so run the risk of getting lost or injured. Also, a doggy bag will have to be carried for dog pooh – yeah, it's natural, but also inconsiderate to leave for other hikers to smell and for their kids to step in. In addition, most dogs almost always will lose a battle against a threatening animal, so there's a price to be paid for your safety.

Many places where you'll hike solve the dilemma for you as dogs aren't allowed on their trails. Dogs are verboten on some Wisconsin state parks trails but usually permitted on those in county forests. Always check with the park ranger before heading to the trail.

If you can bring a dog, make sure it is well behaved and friendly to others. You don't need your dog biting another hiker while unnecessarily defending its family.

Rules of the trail

Ah, the woods or a wide open meadow, peaceful and quiet, not a single soul around for miles. Now you and your children can do whatever you want.

Not so fast.

Act like wild animals on a hike, and you'll destroy the very aspects of the wilds that make them so attractive. Act like wild animals, and you're likely to end up back in civilization, specifically an emergency room. And there are other people around. Just as you would wish them to treat you courteously, so you and your children should do the same for them.

Let's cover how to act civilized out in the wilds.

Minimize damage to your surroundings

When on the trail, follow the maxim of "Leave no trace." Obviously, you shouldn't toss litter on the ground, start rockslides, or pollute water supplies. How much is damage and how much is good-natured exploring is a gray area, of course. Most serious backpackers will say you should never pick up objects, break branches, throw rocks, pick flowers, and so on – the idea is not to disturb the environment at all.

Good luck getting a four-year-old to think like that. The good news is a four-year-old won't be able to throw around many rocks or break many branches.

Still, children from their first hike into the wilderness should be taught to respect nature and to not destroy their environment. While you might overlook a preschooler hurling rocks into a puddle, they can be taught to sniff rather than pick flowers. As they grow older, you can teach them the value of leaving the rock alone. Regardless of age, don't allow children to write on boulders or carve into trees.

Many hikers split over picking berries. To strictly abide by the "minimize damage" principle, you wouldn't pick any berries at all. Kids, however, are likely to find great pleasure in eating black-berries, currants, and thimbleberries as ambling down the trail. Personally, I don't see any problem enjoying a few berries if the long-term payoff is a respect and love for nature. To minimize damage, teach them to only pick berries they can reach from the trail so they don't trample plants or deplete food supplies for animals. They also should only pick what they'll eat.

Collecting is another issue. In national and most state and county parks, taking rocks, flower blossoms and even pine cones is illegal. Picking flowers moves many species, especially if they are rare and native, one step closer to extinction. Archeological ruins are extremely fragile, and even touching them can damage a site.

But on many trails, especially gem trails, collecting is part of the adventure. Use common sense – if the point of the trail is to find materials to collect, such as a gem trail, take judiciously, meaning don't overcollect. Otherwise, leave it there.

Sometimes the trail crosses private land. If so, walking around fields, not through them, always is best or you could damage a farmer's crops.

Pack out what you pack in

Set the example as a parent: Don't litter yourself; whenever stopping, pick up whatever you've dropped; and always require kids to pick up after themselves when they litter. In the spirit of "Leave no trace," try to leave the trail cleaner than you found it, so if you come across litter that's safe to pick up, do so and bring it back to a trash bin in civilization. Given this, you may want to bring a plastic bag to carry out garbage.

Picking up litter doesn't just mean gum and candy wrappers but also some organic materials that take a long time to decompose and aren't likely to be part of the natural environment you're hiking. In particular, these include peanut shells, orange peelings, and eggshells.

Burying litter, by the way, isn't viable. Either animals or erosion soon will dig it up, leaving it scattered around the trail and woods.

Stay on the trail

Hiking off trail means potentially damaging fragile growth. Following this rule not only ensures you minimize damage but is also a matter of safety. Off trail is where kids most likely will encounter dangerous animals and poisonous plants. Not being able to see where they're stepping also increases the likelihood of falling and injuring themselves. Leaving the trail raises the chances of getting lost. Staying on the trail also means staying out of caves, mines or abandoned structures you may encounter. They are usually dangerous places.

Finally, never let children take a shortcut on a switchback trail. Besides putting them on steep ground upon which they could slip, their impatient act will cause the switchback to erode.

Trail dangers

On Bayfield County trails, two common dangers face hikers: ticks and poison ivy/sumac. Both can make your stay at the cabin or your time once back home miserable. Fortunately, both threats are easily avoidable and treatable.

Ticks

One of the greatest dangers comes from the smallest of creatures: ticks. Both the wood and the deer tick are common in the state and can infect people with Lyme disease and much more rarely Rocky Mountain spotted fever.

Ticks usually leap onto people from the top of a grass blade as you brush against it, so walking in the middle of the trail away from high plants is a good idea. Wearing a hat, a long sleeve shirt tucked into pants, and pants tucked into shoes or socks, also will keep ticks off you, though this is not foolproof as they sometimes can hook onto clothing. A tightly woven cloth provides the best protection, however. Children can pick up a tick that has hitchhiked onto the family dog, so outfit Rover and Queenie with a tick-repelling collar.

After hiking into an area where ticks live, you'll want to examine your children's bodies (as well as your own) for them. Check warm, moist areas of the skin, such as under the arms, the groin and head hair. Wearing light-colored clothing helps make the tiny tick easier to spot.

To get rid of a tick that has bitten your child, drip either disinfectant or rubbing alcohol on the bug, so it will loosen its grip. Grip the tick close to its head, slowly pulling it away from the skin. This hopefully will prevent it from releasing saliva that spreads disease. Rather than kill the tick, keep it in a plastic bag so that medical professionals can analyze it should disease symptoms appear. Next, wash the bite area with soap and water then apply antiseptic.

In the days after leaving the woods, also check for signs of disease from ticks. Look for bulls-eye rings, a sign of a Lyme disease. Other symptoms include a large red rash, joint pain, and flu-like symptoms. Indications of Rocky Mountain spotted fever include headache, fever, severe muscle aches, and a spotty rash first on palms and feet soles that spread, all beginning about two days after the bite.

If any of these symptoms appear, seek medical attention immediately. Fortunately, antibiotics exist to cure most tick-related diseases.

Poison ivy/sumac

Often the greatest danger in the wilds isn't our own clumsiness or foolhardiness but various plants we encounter. The good news is that we mostly have to force the encounter with flora. Touching the leaves of either poison ivy or poison sumac in particular results in an itchy, painful rash. Each plant's sticky resin, which causes the reaction, clings to clothing and hair, so you may not have "touched" a leaf, but once your hand runs against the resin on shirt or jeans, you'll probably get the rash.

To avoid touching these plants, you'll need to be able to identify each one. Remember the "Leaves of three, let it be" rule for poison ivy. Besides groups of three leaflets, poison ivy has shiny green leaves that are red in spring and fall. Poison sumac's leaves are not toothed as are non-poisonous sumac, and in autumn their leaves turn scarlet. Be forewarned that even after leaves fall off, poison oak's stems can carry some of the itchy resin.

By staying on the trail and walking down its middle rather than the edges, you are unlikely to come into contact with this pair of irritating plants. That probably is the best preventative. Poison ivy barrier creams also can be helpful, but they only temporarily block the resin. This lulls you into a false sense of safety, and so you may not bother to watch for poison ivy.

To treat poison ivy/sumac, wash the part of the body that has touched the plant with poison ivy soap and cold water. This will erode the oily resin, so it'll be easier to rinse off. If you don't have any of this special soap, plain soap sometimes will work if used within a half-hour of touching the plant. Apply a poison ivy cream and get medical attention immediately. Wearing gloves, remove any clothing (including shoes) that has touched the plants, washing them and the worn gloves right away.

For more about these topics and many others, pick up this author's "Hikes with Tykes: A Practical Guide to Day Hiking with Kids." You also can find tips online at the author's "Hikes with Tykes" blog (*hikeswithtykes.blogspot.com*). Have fun on the trail!

Index

About the Author

Rob Bignell is a long-time hiker, journalist, and author of the popular "Hikes with Tykes" guidebooks and several other titles. He and his son Kieran have been hiking together for the past seven years. Before Kieran, Rob served as an infantryman in the Army National Guard and taught middle school students in New Mexico and Wisconsin. His newspaper work has won several national and state journalism awards, from editorial writing to sports reporting. In 2001, The Prescott Journal, which he served as managing editor of, was named Wisconsin's Weekly Newspaper of the Year. Rob and Kieran live in western Wisconsin.

CHECK OUT THESE OTHER HIKING BOOKS BY ROB BIGNELL

"Headin' to the Cabin" series:
•Day Hiking Trails of Northeast Minnesota (COMING 2015)
•Day Hiking Trails of Northwest Wisconsin

"Hikes with Tykes" series:
•Hikes with Tykes: A Practical Guide to Day Hiking with Children
•Hikes with Tykes: Games and Activities

"Hittin' the Trail":
•Barron County, Wis.
•Burnett County, Wis.
•Crex Meadow Wildlife Area (Wis.)
•Grand Canyon National Park
•Interstate State Park (Minn./Wis.)
•Polk County, Wis.
•Sawyer County, Wis.
•St. Croix National Scenic Riverway

ORDER THEM ONLINE AT:
hikeswithtykes.com/hittinthetrail_home.html

WANT MORE INFO ABOUT FAMILY DAY HIKES?

Follow this book's blog, where you'll find:

Tips on day hiking with kids

Lists of great trails to hike with children

Parents' questions about
day hiking answered

Product reviews

Games and activities for the trail

News about the book series
and author

Visit online at:
hikeswithtykes.blogspot.com

Made in the USA
Middletown, DE
16 May 2023

30678410R00080